U ARE NOT THE RAIN

U ARE NOT THE RAIN

OVERCOMING STIGMAS, EMBRACING EMPATHY

GERAL DEAN

Geral Dean
U Are Not The Rain

Published by Spines
ISBN 979-8-89691-004-6

CONTENTS

PREFACE

Many of us go through life with so much difficulty, while others do so with ease. Sometimes it's not even our struggles that cripple us. It's the struggles of our loved ones. We watch them battle helplessly with their minds, and we wish we could make it go away.

For the sake of compassion, we must also pay mind to non-family or personal relationship members who are struggling with one mental illness or the other all-around the globe.

Whatever the case might be, it wouldn't be too far-fetched to want some understanding in such a harsh world. To not be judged and ridiculed and have some form of support from whatever strange person we come across.

I wrote this book to shed some light on various mental illnesses the society overlooks and undermines.

I chose to expand on mental health because I feel that society needs to give more attention to mental health. After all, it is a fundamental aspect of our lives that we cannot do without entirely.

I have witnessed several mental health cases get mismanaged due to a lack of knowledge and understanding of the condition. I have experienced a mental illness and overcame it.

I want this book to impact several lives and help you understand that mental illnesses are just a condition and not a reason for stigma and ostracization by the public.

I would most importantly like to impact a form of empathy on whoever comes across this book, and perhaps after reading it, you might be able to relate with what you once knew as strange.

I hope that you enjoy reading this book, and I hope that you can learn a lot from it and hopefully overcome your struggles through this.

Stay strong. You got this, and the world is here for you.

INTRODUCTION

The saying "health is wealth" is an all-encompassing statement centered around the health sector, with mental health in the middle. Currently, many individuals are battling with symptoms of a mental health disorder without knowing.

Health is the complete physical, mental, and emotional well-being of an individual, with a complete absence of a diseased state.

A mentally healthy person always seeks opportunities that foster wellness or happiness. The shortfall of psychological well-being results in mental illness, which has become a severe condition.

As we can deduce from the word "mental," these illnesses are conditions that affect the mind. They involve fluctuations in emotions, thoughts, and behavioral changes.

Mental illnesses are associated with stress, social problems, or psychological issues; they take the life out of its preys. They suddenly begin to react differently to life; they may self-isolate or lose interest in what they loved doing or destroy relationships built over the years by actions beyond their control. Conditions like anxiety make you paranoid about certain people in your life, including those very close to you. Patients with anxiety may also hallucinate and experience feelings of abandonment. Gradually, life is taken out; if left untreated, it may result in suicide.

Some years back, mental illness was a sort of stigmatization amongst any group of people. To the commoner, mental health illness was equal to the cases of insane people who had lost their minds and had no hope. A visit to the psychiatrist was always considered a stigma. It made it difficult for people who suffered any degree of mental illness, causing them to withdraw into their shells in a bid to save the little self-esteem they still had. However, they never knew that hiding their condition was a catalyst that sped their mental degradation rate.

This condition of the mind can be considered severe when you experience extreme stress, miserable feelings, and severe emotional and behavioral impairments. It psychologically limits your engagement in physical and social activities.

It's common to experience feelings of sadness once in a while, but it's necessary to know when these feelings are beyond normal. This book sheds more light on some common mental illnesses, detailing the causes, symptoms, and management techniques. Remember, the first step to the solution of a problem is in its identification. The second step is in your admittance. The third step is dialogue. It would be best if mentally ill people learned to speak up.

CHAPTER 1
YOU'RE NOT THE RAIN

Are you feeling overwhelmed and out of control? Maybe you feel like your emotions are dictating your life, or that circumstances are controlling you. You may even be struggling to take back the reins of your mental health. It's time to recognize that while we all will inevitably experience difficult times, it doesn't have to define who we are.

In this chapter, we'll explore the idea that you are not the rain - you are more than your emotions and circumstances. You have the capacity to take control of your mental health and experience true freedom. By understanding that you're more than just a victim of your emotions or surroundings, you can begin to reclaim control of your life.

I had a friend who always seemed to be on the edge. Her emotions were volatile, and she had days where she barely spoke a word. She was often overwhelmed by her feelings as if they were a wild hurricane inside of her that she couldn't control. One day I asked her what was wrong, but all she said was "I'm just not myself lately". I tried to reach out, but she wasn't ready to talk yet. Eventually, I learned it wasn't just short-term sadness; my friend had been struggling with mental health issues for some time now.

Rather than pushing her or trying to make things better immediately, I decided to try and understand what she was going through. I spent some time researching mental health and even read some quotes from famous people who had experienced similar struggles. It was then that I realized how powerful positive thinking can be in dealing with mental health issues.

I started talking to my friend more, trying to encourage her to take care of herself and focus on the things she could control. I told her stories about how other people had used positive thinking to get through tough times, which seemed like a nice way to show her that she wasn't alone in this fight. Gradually, we began finding little ways for her to take back control over her own life and mental health.

We continued talking regularly, and eventually, I saw a change in her attitude. She was still very aware of her mental health struggles, but she was also more accepting of them and less afraid to talk about them.

My friend's journey toward taking control of her own mental health was a long and difficult one, but it taught me an important lesson: that with the right support, there is always hope. You are never defined by your emotions or circumstances. No matter how dark things may seem, you can take back control and reclaim your life. My friend reminded me that even in the harshest storms, we can still be stronger than the rain.

ACKNOWLEDGING DIFFICULT TIMES

We have all experienced times when our emotions seem to be out of control, or when circumstances beyond our control dictate our lives. When we feel overwhelmed and powerless against the events that shape us, it can be difficult to take back the reins of our mental health. But it's important to remember that while we will inevitably experience challenging times, they do not define who we are.

When facing mental health issues, it's essential to acknowledge how tough things can be without judging ourselves for feeling this way. Recognizing these feelings is an important step in taking back control of your life and allowing yourself to move forward. Mental health issues can be complicated and often require more than just a positive attitude to overcome them. The good news is that there are steps you can take to make things easier.

One of the first things we need to do is figure out what triggers our emotions, so we can better manage them in the future. It's also important to practice self-care, as this helps us stay grounded and maintain perspective during difficult times. Finally, understanding the immense power of positive thinking can help us find hope in any situation and build resilience against mental health struggles.

It's crucial for us to remind ourselves that no matter how intense our emotions or circumstances may seem, we are more than our feelings. Though it can be hard to believe, you are not defined by your emotions or the events that occur in your life. Just like a storm passes and eventually gives way to sunshine, so too will any mental health struggles provide an opportunity for growth and resilience.

I recently experienced this firsthand when my best friend went through a difficult period of depression. I could feel her fear and despair as she grappled with her own thoughts and emotions, seemingly unable to control anything that was happening around her. It was heartbreaking to see someone so close to me struggle with something they felt powerless against. But despite all these challenges, I still believed in her and that she could make it through this tough time and regain control of her life.

Throughout history, many famous people have spoken out about their own mental health struggles and how they overcame them. Reading these quotes can be an inspiring way to remind ourselves that we are not alone in our journey and that there is hope, even in the darkest times.

For example, John Dryden said, "There's pleasure in being mad which none but madmen know". This quote shows us that while it may seem like madness at first, there is a certain freedom that comes with embracing our inner turmoil. Winston Churchill also reminded us of the importance of resilience when facing mental health issues: "If you're going through hell, keep going". This emphasizes the power of positive thinking and how it can help us move forward despite any hardship or fear that might be stopping us.

Eleanor Roosevelt was famously quoted as saying, "You must do the thing you think you cannot do". This quote is a powerful reminder of how facing our fears can be one of the most important steps we take in overcoming mental health struggles. Author Marya Hornbacher said "Inside each of us is a wild thing. Don't try to stifle it - nurture it and accept its presence." This quote reminds us that our emotions can be powerful allies in our journey to reclaim control of our mental health.

By embracing them instead of trying to ignore or suppress them, we can learn how to use them as tools for growth and self-discovery.

Dan Millman said "You don't have to control your thoughts. You just have to stop letting them control you." This quote is a reminder that although we can't always control our thoughts, we do have power over how we react to them. We can choose to let them be or take action and refuse to be defined by our mental health struggles.

William James gave us insight into the importance of understanding ourselves: "The greatest discovery of any generation is that a human being can alter his life by altering his attitude". This quote highlights how crucial it is to not only recognize triggers and practice self-care but also to understand our own thoughts and feelings so that we can begin to take control of our lives. All these famous quotes about mental health provide an inspiring way for us to start our journey toward healing and reclaiming control of our lives.

In the past, the government has made efforts to address mental health issues in a variety of ways. For example, they have implemented programs that would provide resources and support to those struggling with mental illness, such as the Mental Health Parity Act of 1996 (MHPA), which required insurance companies to cover mental health services at a comparable level to other medical treatments. These efforts have been beneficial for those who are able to access them, but unfortunately, not everyone is able to access this kind of help.

Those behind bars are especially vulnerable when it comes to mental health; many prisons and jails lack adequate resources and personnel to properly care for inmates with serious mental illnesses. In addition, incarceration often compounds existing mental health problems due to the isolation and stress associated with being in prison. A recent study conducted by the National Alliance on Mental Illness found that more than half of inmates in U.S. prisons suffer from some form of mental illness - a much higher rate than among the general population. Sadly, this means that many individuals are not getting the help they need while in custody and instead face further deterioration of their condition.

Addressing mental health issues in prisons and jails is a complex issue, but there are certain steps that can be taken to help ensure that those behind bars are able to access the resources they need. One such step is increasing training for correctional officers so that they can better identify and understand mental illness.

Additionally, providing access to therapy, medications, and other services tailored specifically for inmates with mental illness would go a long way toward addressing this pressing problem. Finally, making sure that parolees have access to resources upon their release is key; these individuals already face an uphill battle in readjusting to society after spending time in prison, and having access to meaningful mental health care could make all the difference in ensuring successful reintegration into their communities.

Taking back the reins of mental health can be a daunting journey, but it is one we must take if we want to take control of our lives and thrive. Although our emotions and circumstances are everchanging and out of our control, we have power over how we react to them. We can choose to let them define us or use them as tools for growth.

Just like the rain passes and eventually gives way to sunshine, so too will any mental health struggles provide an opportunity for growth and resilience. You may feel powerless against your own thoughts sometimes but you are strong enough to overcome these challenges. Remember: you're not the rain - you're in charge of your future.

Some other points about

"ACKNOWLEDGING DIFFICULT TIMES"

Facing the Storm:

It's natural to want to avoid the feelings that come with difficult times—sadness, fear, anger, or frustration. We might bury ourselves in distractions or tell ourselves we're fine when we're not. But difficult times don't just go away on their own; they often build up, like dark clouds on the horizon. When you acknowledge them, you give yourself permission to feel and release the tension, instead of carrying it with you for longer than you need to.

Reflection Prompt:

Think about a time recently when you felt overwhelmed, stressed, or in emotional pain. Write about how you responded to those feelings. Did you try to avoid them, or were you able to acknowledge them?

What was your storm like? Describe the experience in detail. Were there specific triggers or circumstances that made it harder to face?

Sitting with Discomfort:

Acknowledging difficult times doesn't mean solving them right away. Sometimes, just sitting with the discomfort is all we can do. And that's okay. Sitting with tough emotions can be uncomfortable, but it also allows you to understand them better. When you give yourself the space to experience your feelings without judgment, you can find clarity in the storm.

Reflection Prompt:

Write about a time when you sat with your emotions instead of pushing them away. What did it feel like? How did your body respond—did you feel tension, exhaustion, or relief?

Now, imagine doing this in the future. The next time a difficult moment arises, how might you allow yourself to sit with those emotions, even if just for a little while?

Acknowledging vs. Fixing:

Sometimes, when we face difficult times, our instinct is to fix everything right away. But not all problems can be solved immediately, and not all pain can be "fixed." Acknowledging tough moments doesn't mean you have to find a solution right away—it just means recognizing they exist and allowing yourself to feel them. Solutions may come in time, but the act of simply acknowledging gives you strength and presence in the moment.

Reflection Prompt:

Is there a situation in your life right now that feels difficult but doesn't have an easy solution? Write about it honestly—what emotions come up when you think about it?

Can you separate the need to fix the situation from the need to acknowledge it? How does it feel to allow the problem to exist without rushing to solve it?

Recognizing Strength in Vulnerability:

Acknowledging difficult times isn't a sign of weakness—it's a sign of strength. By facing your struggles, you show courage. There is power in vulnerability, in admitting that things are hard, and in allowing yourself to feel deeply. When you acknowledge pain, you take the first step toward healing and growth.

Reflection Prompt:

Think about a time when you were vulnerable with yourself or someone else about a difficult time. How did it feel to open up? What was the response?

If you haven't been able to be vulnerable yet, what might it look like to acknowledge your difficult feelings? How can you gently allow yourself to be open and honest?

Moving Through the Storm:

Acknowledging difficult times doesn't make them disappear, but it does help you start the journey through them. Once you recognize the rain, you can begin to navigate through it. This doesn't mean forcing yourself to be "okay" too soon, but rather allowing yourself to move at your own pace, one step at a time. Healing is a process, not a destination.

Reflection Prompt:

What are small, manageable steps you can take when you're facing a difficult time? Write about one thing you might do when things feel overwhelming. Maybe it's reaching out to someone, taking a break, or simply acknowledging that today was hard and that's okay.

How can you remind yourself that progress is made in small, meaningful ways, and that you don't have to rush your healing?

Acknowledging difficult times is a courageous act. By recognizing your struggles, you are giving yourself the gift of self-awareness and acceptance. You are not the rain, but acknowledging the rain is how you begin to understand it. Let yourself be present with your emotions, knowing that by facing the storm, you are building resilience and strength. You are allowing space for healing, even in the hardest moments.

BATTLING MENTAL ILLNESSES: AN INSPIRING LOOK INTO THE LIVES OF A FEW

Mental illnesses are often perceived as an invisible enemy, yet they can be incredibly powerful and relentless. Many have faced these challenges with strength and courage, refusing to succumb to them. Here we will explore the lives of a few extraordinary individuals who battled mental illness head-on and still managed to make a huge impact on the world – proving that anything is possible when you put your mind to it.

Napoleon Bonaparte, the French military leader who rose to become Emperor of France, was a man whose life was marked by great successes and tragedies. He is best known for his conquests on the battlefield and is considered one of the most successful military strategists of all time. However, during his later years, he faced debilitating bouts of depression that threatened to consume him.

Bonaparte had experienced periods of extreme mood swings since childhood but it wasn't until he reached middle age that these episodes became steadily more frequent and severe. His mental health deteriorated further after his exile from France in 1815. During this time, he sought solace in alcohol but also developed an interest in philosophy which provided some comfort during this difficult period of his life.

The story of Winston Churchill has often been cited as a prime example of how one can live with and overcome the bipolar disorder. Churchill suffered from depression during most of his adult life but he found ways to cope with it successfully. He sought solace in hobbies such as painting and writing, which helped him to focus on something other than his own mental health issues. Churchill was also an avid reader and this enabled him to keep informed and maintain his sharp wit.

There's a famous person out there who has become a beacon of hope and inspiration for many who have dealt with mental health issues. Having been through his own struggles, this individual is now using their platform to bring attention to the issue of mental health and raise awareness about it.

In 2011, after undergoing an intense evaluation at the McLean Hospital in Belmont, Massachusetts, this person was diagnosed with Borderline Personality Disorder (BPD). Armed with this newfound knowledge and understanding of BPD, they embarked on a journey to break down stigmas associated with having a mental illness.

Since then, he has worked tirelessly to spread awareness about the importance of caring for one's mental health. From speaking out publicly about their struggle and advocating for proper treatment for those with mental illness, to partnering with organizations like Project 375, this person has become a leading voice in the fight for mental health awareness.

Today, this individual is an inspiration to many, showing them that it's ok to have a mental illness and that recovery is possible. Their story proves that if you face your fears head-on and equip yourself with knowledge and understanding, you can find hope and healing on the other side.

In doing so, he is helping to break down the stigma associated with mental illness and make it easier for everyone to access the care they need. As they put it, "One person can make a difference". Indeed, Brandon Marshall has become that one person making a real difference in the world of mental health advocacy. He should be commended for his courage and dedication to this cause.

Another famous media personality has recently come forward and shared their story of depression with the world. After months of darkness, they emerged as a strong individual who is ready to take on any obstacle that comes their way.

This person's social media posts revealed the difficulties they faced in life, including loss of appetite, increased desire for alcohol, and insomnia. The pictures they shared online showed a striking contrast between their healthy self and the struggles they were going through at that time.

Depression caused this person immense distress; it completely changed their normal habits, lifestyle, and attitude toward life. Eating was something they could no longer enjoy due to the lack of appetite it caused, and alcohol served as a temporary escape from reality, but unfortunately, it only made matters worse.

Despite the darkness they endured in the past months, this person stayed strong and sought help from professionals to overcome their depression. They expressed gratitude for being able to get the treatment that helped them find joy again and brought back the beautiful smile on their face.

The inspiring story of this person should be an example to us all: that recovery is possible if we are willing to make the necessary changes in our lives. We can all admire their journey, and find hope in knowing that anything can be conquered with strength and resilience – including depression. This person is none other than Olivia Culpo.

Another famous pop star has been open about her struggles with mental health over the years. Growing up in a family where both parents had mental health diagnoses, this pop star was at an increased risk of developing a mental illness themselves. Her father was diagnosed with schizophrenia and bipolar disorder, while her mother suffered from an eating disorder.

At a young age, she began to struggle with binge eating and was financially responsible for the family. She gained weight quickly and felt ashamed of how she looked which lead to suicidal thoughts when she was just nine years old. In order to cope with the pressures of life, she began self-medicating with alcohol and cocaine.

However, despite the odds stacked against her, this pop star was able to get help and become an advocate for mental health awareness. Their 2013 hit single 'Heart Attack' speaks of their journey, and is just one example of how they are using their platform to spread hope around the world.

This pop star is none other than Demi Lovato, who continues to inspire millions around the globe with her powerful story. Her bravery and courage have empowered countless people to know that life can be better.

Lastly, we turn our focus to Sylvia Plath – an American poet whose life was tragically cut short due to her struggle with clinical depression. Plath wrote extensively about this condition in her work and often described it in vivid detail. She also bravely sought treatment for her illness but eventually resorted to suicide at just 30 years old.

Plath's story is a tragic reminder of the power of mental illness and how far it can reach. Despite her immense talent and courage, she was unable to outrun this invisible enemy. Her works are a tribute to her graceful struggle with mental illness and her powerful legacy lives on today through her work as an author and poet.

Paulette Wilkie, a 56-year-old woman with schizophrenia, was found dead in the bitter cold behind Ben's Deli – a sandwich shop she frequented. It was too late to trigger an emergency homeless plan by the county as temperatures had not dropped to 20 degrees or below for two consecutive days. People who knew Wilkie said she would not have gone into a shelter anyway.

Wilkie had been in and out of local community mental health centers for more than 20 years and had lived in a group home until last year when she stopped taking her medication and was asked to leave. But Wilkie's father said his daughter didn't like to take her pills. Mental health officials told him she couldn't move back into the home until she got back on her medication and was clean.

The owners of Anthony's Pizza and Ben's Deli saw a sharp decline in Wilkie's mental health before her death - she had stopped bathing, was losing weight, and customers were leaving the pizza shop as her smell was too strong.

Could Wilkie's death have been prevented? Sadly, yes. We must ask ourselves why this woman was homeless in the first place and what can be done to ensure no more tragedies like this happen again. We owe it to Paulette Wilkie – and each other – to make sure this doesn't happen again.

Let's start the conversation now. What can we do to help those who are homeless? How can we make sure everyone has a warm place to sleep when temperatures dip dangerously low? Let's find solutions so no more lives are lost due to homelessness. It's time for us all to take action. Together we can make a difference. Let's do this - for Paulette Wilkie and everyone else we may have the power to help.

Mental illness can contribute to homelessness in a number of ways. People with mental illness may have difficulty finding and maintaining employment, which can lead to financial instability and ultimately homelessness. They may also have difficulty managing their symptoms and engaging in self-care, which can lead to difficulties in relationships and social support. Additionally, people with mental illness may have difficulty accessing and navigating the healthcare and social service systems, which can make it harder for them to get the help they need.

Homelessness is a complex issue with many contributing factors, and addressing it requires a multifaceted approach that includes efforts to address mental health, housing, employment, and social support. It is important for people with mental illness to have access to high-quality mental health care, supportive housing options, and other social and economic supports to help them maintain stability and improve their quality of life.

These stories illustrate that even in the face of great adversity, there is hope for those struggling with mental illnesses. Although these battles may seem insurmountable at times, we can take comfort in knowing that no matter how dark it gets, there is always light at the end of the tunnel. By learning from their stories, we can strive to create a more compassionate and understanding world for those fighting mental illnesses.

Mental illness can feel like a relentless battle, but within this struggle, there are countless stories of resilience, strength, and hope. People from all walks of life face mental health challenges, yet many find ways to confront their illness with courage and grace. This chapter shines a light on a few inspiring individuals who have turned their battles with mental illness into journeys of self-discovery and empowerment. Their stories remind us that while mental illness can be incredibly difficult, it doesn't define a person's potential for healing, growth, and success.

The Story of John: Rising from the Depths of Depression

John was 25 when he first realized that his constant sadness wasn't just a passing mood—it was depression. At his lowest, he struggled to get out of bed, lost interest in things he once loved, and felt isolated from everyone around him. For years, John hid his depression, fearing the stigma of seeking help. He thought he had to handle it on his own. But as the weight of his mental health challenges grew, he made the brave decision to reach out for support.

With therapy, medication, and the encouragement of loved ones, John began to see light again. He wasn't instantly cured, but he learned how to manage his depression and prioritize self-care. One of the most powerful tools in his recovery was learning to express his feelings openly and honestly. John began journaling his thoughts and emotions, which helped him process the pain he had carried for so long.

Today, John shares his story publicly to encourage others not to wait in silence. He speaks at schools and organizations about the importance of seeking help and the strength it takes to confront mental illness. His journey shows that while depression can feel all-consuming, taking small, courageous steps toward healing can change everything.

Sophia's Battle with Anxiety: Finding Strength in Vulnerability

Sophia had always been a perfectionist, which made her battle with anxiety all the more challenging. Throughout her teen years and into her 20s, she experienced constant worry, panic attacks, and a relentless fear of failure. Her anxiety was so overwhelming that she began to avoid social situations, worried that others would see her unravel. She hid her panic attacks from her family and friends, determined to maintain the image of someone who had it all together.

It wasn't until her late 20s that Sophia realized she couldn't continue living In secrecy. One day, after a particularly intense panic attack, she confided in a close friend about her struggles. The act of opening up felt like a massive weight had been lifted. Her friend's compassion and understanding helped Sophia realize that she didn't have to battle anxiety alone.

Sophia sought help from a therapist who specialized in anxiety disorders, and she began practicing mindfulness and meditation. Through these tools, Sophia learned to recognize the early signs of anxiety and manage her panic attacks more effectively. She also learned that vulnerability is a form of strength. Now, she openly talks about her anxiety, showing others that it's okay to not have everything under control.

Sophia's journey is a testament to the power of vulnerability and self-acceptance. By embracing her anxiety and learning to manage it, she transformed her life—and she continues to inspire others to seek help without shame.

Maria's Journey Through Bipolar Disorder: From Chaos to Stability

For years, Maria's life felt like a roller coaster of extreme highs and devastating lows. Diagnosed with bipolar disorder in her early 30s, she experienced intense periods of mania, where she would feel euphoric, take risky actions, and push her mind and body to the limit. These episodes would inevitably be followed by crushing depression, leaving her unable to function. For a long time, Maria felt trapped in this cycle, unsure of how to find balance.

When Maria finally sought professional help, she began a journey of learning how to live with bipolar disorder, rather than letting it control her. Medication helped stabilize her mood swings, but it was therapy that allowed Maria to rebuild her life. She learned the importance of routine, sleep, and staying connected to her support system. She also discovered her passion for painting, which became a vital outlet for expressing her emotions and navigating her mental health journey.

Maria's openness about her bipolar disorder has empowered others in her community to seek help for their own struggles. She volunteers at mental health organizations, sharing her story to show that stability and joy are possible, even for those living with bipolar disorder. Her message is clear: mental illness doesn't have to define your life, and with the right support, you can find balance and fulfillment.

James: Overcoming PTSD, One Step at a Time

James, a military veteran, struggled with Post-Traumatic Stress Disorder (PTSD) after serving in combat. The nightmares, flashbacks, and constant hypervigilance made it impossible for him to adjust to civilian life. He found himself avoiding crowded spaces, plagued by intrusive memories of his time in the field. For years, James felt disconnected from his family and friends, believing that no one could understand what he was going through.

Eventually, a fellow veteran encouraged James to seek treatment. He began trauma-focused therapy and was introduced to eye movement desensitization and reprocessing (EMDR), a therapy that helped him process his traumatic memories. Though the road to recovery was long, James slowly started to regain control of his life. He learned coping strategies to manage his symptoms and found solace in connecting with other veterans who shared similar experiences.

Today, James uses his story to help other veterans cope with PTSD. He advocates for mental health awareness in the military community, emphasizing that seeking help is a sign of strength, not weakness. His resilience and dedication to healing have transformed his life, showing that even the deepest wounds can heal with time, care, and support.

Strength in the Struggle

The individuals in this chapter—John, Sophia, Maria, and James—are just a few examples of people who have faced immense challenges with mental illness and found their way to healing and strength. Their stories remind us that while the journey can be difficult, it is possible to live fulfilling, meaningful lives despite mental health struggles. Each of them demonstrates the power of resilience, the importance of seeking help, and the courage it takes to confront mental illness head-on.

These stories also remind us that mental illness is not a weakness or a failure; it is part of the human experience. By sharing these journeys, we hope to inspire others to take their own steps toward healing, knowing that they are not alone and that there is always hope, even in the darkest of times.

CHAPTER 2
ASSESSING YOUR MENTAL HEALTH A PRECISE DIAGNOSIS AND BEYOND

Self-assessment is an important first step to understanding and managing your mental health. In this chapter, you will gain knowledge of the common symptoms of mental illness, the causes of such illnesses, the consequences of denial, and how best to manage them. Through a precise diagnosis and a good understanding of mental health, you can make informed decisions about taking charge of your own well-being.

Assessing mental health is a crucial step in understanding and addressing one's psychological well-being. A precise diagnosis can help identify specific conditions and guide appropriate treatment, but mental health assessment goes beyond just pinpointing a disorder. It involves a comprehensive evaluation of your emotional, psychological, and social functioning. This chapter explores the process of mental health assessment, the importance of accurate diagnosis, and the steps you can take to understand and manage your mental health effectively.

Understanding the Assessment Process:

Mental health assessment typically begins with a thorough evaluation by a mental health professional. This process often includes:

1. **Clinical Interviews**: The clinician conducts structured or semi-structured interviews to gather information about your symptoms, history, and current functioning. This can involve discussing your feelings, behaviors, and any life events that may impact your mental health.
2. **Self-Report Questionnaires**: These are standardized tools used to assess various aspects of mental health, such as depression, anxiety, and stress. They help quantify your experiences and provide insights into the severity and frequency of symptoms.
3. **Behavioral Observations:**The clinician may observe your behavior and interactions during sessions to understand how symptoms manifest in real life and how they affect your daily functioning.
4. **Psychological Testing:**In some cases, more formal psychological tests may be used to assess cognitive functions, personality traits, or specific mental health disorders. These tests provide additional data to support the diagnostic process.

Reflection Prompt:

Think about your recent experiences with mental health assessments, if any. How did you feel about the process? Did you find it helpful in understanding your mental health? Write about your thoughts and any concerns you have regarding mental health evaluations.

The Importance of Accurate Diagnosis:

An accurate diagnosis is essential for effective treatment. It helps identify the specific mental health condition you may be experiencing, guiding the choice of appropriate interventions. A precise diagnosis can:

1. **Guide Treatment**: Knowing the exact condition allows for targeted treatment strategies, such as medication, therapy, or lifestyle changes.
2. **Identify Co-occurring Conditions:**Many people experience more than one mental health issue simultaneously. A thorough assessment helps uncover co-occurring conditions, ensuring a holistic treatment approach.
3. **Measure Progress:**An accurate diagnosis provides a baseline against which treatment progress can be measured. This helps track improvements and make necessary adjustments to the treatment plan.

Reflection Prompt:

Consider how an accurate diagnosis has impacted your treatment or understanding of your mental health. If you have not yet received a diagnosis, how might having one change your approach to managing your mental health?

Beyond Diagnosis: Comprehensive Management

While diagnosis is crucial, managing mental health involves more than just identifying a condition. Effective management includes:

1. **Personalized Treatment Plan:**Based on your diagnosis, a mental health professional will create a tailored treatment plan that may include therapy, medication, lifestyle changes, or a combination of these. The plan

should be regularly reviewed and adjusted based on your progress and any changing needs.

2. **Self-Care Practices:**Incorporating self-care into your daily routine can greatly impact your mental health. This includes activities that promote well-being, such as exercise, healthy eating, mindfulness, and sufficient sleep.
3. **Support Systems:**Building a support network of friends, family, or support groups can provide emotional support and practical assistance. Having people who understand and support you can be invaluable in managing mental health.
4. **Ongoing Monitoring:**Regular follow-ups with your mental health professional help track your progress, address any new symptoms or concerns, and adjust your treatment plan as needed.

The Role of Self-Advocacy:

Being an active participant in your mental health care is essential. Self-advocacy involves understanding your condition, expressing your needs, and working collaboratively with your healthcare provider. It also means being proactive about your treatment and seeking help when needed.

Reflection Prompt:

Reflect on how you advocate for your own mental health. Are there areas where you feel confident in your self-advocacy? Are there aspects where you could improve? Write about any steps you can take to become a more active participant in your mental health care.

Assessing your mental health involves more than just receiving a diagnosis; it's about understanding your overall well-being and actively engaging in your treatment and self-care. Accurate diagnosis provides a foundation for effective treatment, but managing mental health requires a comprehensive approach that includes personalized care, self-care practices, support systems, and ongoing monitoring. By being proactive and involved in your mental health journey, you can take meaningful steps toward well-being and resilience.

IMPORTANCE OF A PRECISE DIAGNOSIS

It is essential to have an accurate assessment of your mental health in order to manage it effectively. Self-assessment can be helpful as it allows you to look closely at your emotions, thoughts, and behavior, enabling you to identify any changes or inconsistencies that may indicate a problem. It also gives you the opportunity to examine how these developments are impacting your overall well-being and could even lead to early detection of a mental condition before it becomes more serious.

Making sure that you receive an accurate diagnosis for any potential mental illness is very important. Without this knowledge, it's difficult to take appropriate action when managing the problem – whether it be through therapy, medication, lifestyle changes, or a combination of all three. Furthermore, not receiving treatment can lead to an exacerbation of symptoms and can also cause other illnesses as well.

However, it's not always easy to recognize the signs and symptoms of mental illness, especially if you have never experienced them before. That is why it is important to be mindful of any changes in your behavior and emotional state that seem out of character for yourself. Taking note of how you are feeling on a regular basis is key for self-assessment – writing down any negative thoughts, feelings, or behaviors and looking at their frequency can be useful too. It may also help to talk about these experiences with people close to you who know you best so they can give you an honest opinion.

When it comes to the actual diagnosis, seeking the help of a mental health professional can be beneficial. They will likely ask you questions about your symptoms and may do some tests to ascertain if there is an underlying problem. It is important for you to be open and honest throughout this process so that the practitioner can get a proper understanding of what's going on. Depending on their findings, they may refer you to other specialists such as psychiatrists or psychologists who are better equipped to treat certain conditions than general practitioners.

A precise diagnosis In mental health is crucial for several reasons. It enables healthcare professionals to create a targeted treatment plan tailored specifically to the identified condition. This specificity ensures that interventions are appropriate and effective, avoiding unnecessary treatments that might arise from an incorrect or vague diagnosis. Accurate diagnosis also provides clarity on the symptoms of a mental health condition, helping individuals recognize and monitor their experiences more effectively. Understanding the exact nature of their condition allows for better symptom management and coping strategies.

Moreover, a precise diagnosis helps identify co-occurring conditions, which are common in mental health, ensuring that all aspects of an individual's mental health are addressed in a comprehensive manner. This holistic approach to treatment can prevent issues from being overlooked and ensures that the care plan is integrated.

An accurate diagnosis also facilitates the tracking of progress and adjustment of treatment plans. It allows healthcare providers to measure improvements and make informed changes if necessary. This ongoing adjustment helps in optimizing treatment and achieving better outcomes.

Furthermore, a precise diagnosis can reduce stigma and promote understanding. By clearly defining a mental health condition, it helps distinguish it from general stress or personality traits, leading to a better understanding and acceptance of the condition. It also provides opportunities for education, which can foster a more supportive environment.

In addition, it guides support systems, informing family members, friends, and caregivers about the condition and how they can best offer support. It helps in connecting individuals with relevant support groups and resources that align with their specific needs.

Overall, an accurate diagnosis enhances quality of life by providing a clearer understanding of one's mental health, which leads to more effective self-management and personal growth. It empowers individuals by giving them direction and clarity in their mental health journey.

SYMPTOMS OF MENTAL ILLNESSES

Mental illnesses are serious conditions that can greatly affect a person's life. It is essential to recognize the signs of mental health issues and seek help as soon as possible. There is no single symptom or set of symptoms that can diagnose a mental illness, however, there are some common indicators that could signal the need for further evaluation by a professional.

One of the most common symptoms associated with certain mental health issues is changes in mood. These changes can range from periods of high energy and excitement to feelings of sadness, emptiness, or hopelessness. Other changes in emotions such as increased irritability, quickness to anger, or loss of interest in things one normally enjoys may also be signs of deeper emotional disturbances.

Those struggling with mental health problems may also experience an inability to concentrate, increased forgetfulness, or difficulty making decisions. This can lead to a decline in school or work performance and make day-to-day activities more difficult and challenging.

Changes in behavior are another sign of potential mental health issues. Those experiencing emotional disturbances may begin taking part in risky behaviors such as substance abuse or engaging in risky sexual activity. On the other hand, those who become withdrawn may isolate themselves from friends, family, and social activities that they once enjoyed. In addition to changes in behavior, alterations in sleep patterns and appetite could be indicative of deeper underlying mental health concerns.

Thoughts of self-harm or suicide are one of the more serious symptoms of mental health problems and should always be taken seriously. Such thoughts can range from mild to severe, but any such expression should be taken as a warning sign that immediate help is needed.

Hallucinations, delusions, and paranoia are all symptoms of certain mental health issues that can cause extreme discomfort and make it difficult to carry out everyday tasks. Hallucinations involve the perception of sensory information that is not actually present. This can include hearing voices or seeing images that no one else sees. Delusions involve strange beliefs that have no basis in reality, such as believing someone is out to get them when there is no evidence of this. Paranoia involves feelings of suspicion or mistrust towards others without any valid reason.

People experiencing these symptoms often feel overwhelmed and confused by their own perceptions or sense of reality, which can be very daunting and distressing. It is important to recognize these symptoms and seek help from a qualified professional who can provide support and guidance in managing them.

People with mental health conditions may also experience changes in their ability to think clearly and focus on the tasks at hand. This can lead to difficulty concentrating, making decisions, or remembering things–all common signs that something more serious may be going on beneath the surface. People with mental health issues may also start exhibiting irrational behaviors such as speaking in a different tone than usual or being more aggressive towards others than they normally would be.

One's physical well-being may also be affected by mental illness. This can result in a decline in energy levels, headaches or stomachaches, or even unexplained aches and pains throughout the body. Experiencing one or more of these physical symptoms could signal underlying emotional issues such as depression or anxiety disorders.

Mental health issues can cause great distress for those who are suffering and it is important to recognize these signs early on before things become worse. If you or someone close to you have displayed any of the symptoms above, it is important to reach out for help. Even if the symptoms are mild, professional evaluation can be beneficial in identifying underlying issues and developing a plan of action.

The symptoms of mental illnesses vary widely depending on the specific condition. Here are some common symptoms associated with various mental health disorders:

Depression:

- Persistent sadness or low mood
- Loss of interest or pleasure in activities once enjoyed
- Changes in appetite or weight
- Sleep disturbances (insomnia or oversleeping)
- Fatigue or lack of energy
- Feelings of worthlessness or excessive guilt
- Difficulty concentrating or making decisions
- Thoughts of death or suicide

Anxiety Disorders:

- Excessive worry or fear
- Restlessness or feeling on edge
- Muscle tension
- Rapid heartbeat or sweating
- Shortness of breath
- Avoidance of certain situations due to fear
- Difficulty relaxing or calming down

Bipolar Disorder:

- Extreme mood swings between mania and depression
- Mania: Elevated or irritable mood, increased energy, racing thoughts, impulsive behavior
- Depression: Symptoms similar to those listed under depression
- Impaired judgment and risky behaviors during manic episodes

Schizophrenia:

- Delusions (false beliefs)
- Hallucinations (hearing or seeing things that are not there)
- Disorganized thinking and speech
- Flat affect or reduced emotional expression
- Withdrawal from social interactions
- Impaired functioning in daily life

Obsessive-Compulsive Disorder (OCD):

- Obsessions: Persistent, intrusive thoughts or urges
- Compulsions: Repetitive behaviors or mental acts performed to reduce anxiety or prevent a feared event
- Significant distress or impairment caused by obsessions and compulsions

Post-Traumatic Stress Disorder (PTSD):

- Flashbacks or intrusive memories of a traumatic event
- Nightmares or distressing dreams
- Avoidance of reminders or triggers associated with the trauma
- Hypervigilance or heightened startle response
- Emotional numbness or difficulty experiencing positive emotions

Borderline Personality Disorder (BPD):

- Intense, unstable emotions and relationships
- Fear of abandonment
- Impulsive behaviors (e.g., spending sprees, substance abuse)
- Self-harming behaviors or suicidal thoughts
- Chronic feelings of emptiness
- Difficulty with self-image and identity

Attention-Deficit/Hyperactivity Disorder (ADHD):

- Inattention: Difficulty sustaining focus, making careless mistakes, forgetfulness
- Hyperactivity: Excessive fidgeting, restlessness, difficulty staying seated

- Impulsivity: Difficulty waiting turns, interrupting others, making hasty decisions

Eating Disorders:

- Anorexia Nervosa: Extreme restriction of food intake, intense fear of gaining weight, distorted body image
- Bulimia Nervosa: Recurrent episodes of binge eating followed by compensatory behaviors (e.g., vomiting, excessive exercise)
- Binge-Eating Disorder: Recurrent episodes of eating large quantities of food without compensatory behaviors

These symptoms can vary in intensity and duration and may overlap between different disorders. It's important to consult a mental health professional for an accurate diagnosis and appropriate treatment if you or someone you know is experiencing these

CAUSES OF MENTAL ILLNESS

Mental illnesses are a diverse group of disorders that affect an individual's thoughts, emotions, and behaviors. Mental illnesses can range from mild to severe and can be temporary or long-lasting. While there is no single cause for mental illness, a variety of biological, psychological, and environmental factors play a role in the development of mental health conditions.

1. BIOLOGICAL FACTORS

Mental illness can be caused by a number of biological factors, including genetic predisposition, chemical imbalances in the brain, neurological conditions, and trauma.

❖ *GENETIC PREDISPOSITION*

Mental illness can sometimes be linked to a person's genetic makeup, which can predispose them to develop certain mental health conditions. While genetics are not the only factor that contributes to the development of mental illness, they can play an important role in determining an individual's susceptibility.

For instance, if one or both of a person's parents have been diagnosed with a mental illness, the child is at an increased risk of developing the same disorder. This is because certain genes that code for mental illness may be inherited from parents and passed down through generations. Additionally, environmental factors such as trauma, stress, and poverty can further increase the chances of a person developing a psychiatric disorder.

Further complicating this matter is that there are many different genes related to mental illnesses, some of which may interact with each other or with environmental factors in order to produce symptoms. For example, some gene variants related to schizophrenia are associated with increased risk when exposed to certain stressful events in life. It is also possible that more than one gene variant can contribute to the development of certain conditions.

However, it should be noted that just because someone has a genetic predisposition for mental illness does not mean that they will automatically develop the condition. The combination of genes and environmental factors needs to be present in order for an individual to experience psychiatric symptoms.

Born in 1946, Kay Redfield Jamison grew up in an environment with high expectations and frequent relocations. While Jamison was highly intelligent, she also suffered from severe depression throughout her childhood, adolescence, and adult life.

It wasn't until 1985 that Jamison finally identified her family's history of manic-depressive illness as a possible cause for her mental health struggles. This realization led to further research into the genetic factors associated with bipolar disorder - a topic on which she has become an expert throughout the years.

Jamison's extensive work in this field has shed light on how particular gene variants may influence susceptibility to bipolar disorder and other psychiatric conditions. She believes that additional research into genetics will continue to be vital in order to understand how biology can shape our mental health experiences both positively and negatively and improve treatments for those who suffer from psychiatric disorders.

Today, Kay Redfield Jamison is one of the world's leading authors on mood disorders and mental health issues in general. She is also a professor at Johns Hopkins University School of Medicine, where she has published multiple books about her own journey with bipolar disorder as well as its potential genetic links. Her work continues to inspire countless individuals around the globe who are struggling with similar symptoms or trying to better understand their own personal battles with mental illness.

Genetic predisposition refers also to an increased likelihood of developing a mental health condition due to one's genetic makeup. While genetics alone do not determine if someone will develop a mental illness, they play a significant role in increasing the risk. Certain mental health disorders, such as schizophrenia, bipolar disorder, and depression, tend to run in families, indicating that genes can contribute to the risk. Research has identified specific genes linked to these conditions, though the exact mechanisms remain complex and not fully understood.

Genetic predisposition interacts with environmental factors to influence mental health. For instance, someone with a genetic risk for depression may be more likely to develop the condition if they experience stressful life events or trauma. This interaction highlights that having a genetic predisposition does not guarantee the development of a mental illness but increases vulnerability.

Many mental health conditions are influenced by multiple genes, each contributing a small amount to the overall risk. This polygenic nature means that no single gene is solely responsible, but rather a combination of genetic factors can increase susceptibility. Family history of mental illness can indicate a genetic predisposition; if close relatives have experienced mental health disorders, an individual may be at higher risk. However, family history alone is not a definitive predictor, as lifestyle, environment, and personal experiences also play crucial roles.

Advances in genetic research have enhanced our understanding of how genes contribute to mental health. Genome-wide association studies (GWAS) have identified various genetic variants associated with mental health conditions. While genetic research continues to reveal potential risk factors, mental health is influenced by a combination of genetic, biological, psychological, and environmental factors.

Understanding genetic predisposition can help in developing personalized treatment plans and preventive strategies. For individuals with a family history of mental illness, early intervention or proactive mental health monitoring may be beneficial. Additionally, genetic insights can guide research into targeted therapies and interventions tailored to individual genetic profiles. Overall, while genetic predisposition is an important aspect of mental health, it is only one part of a broader picture that includes genetic, environmental, and personal factors.

❖ *BRAIN CHEMISTRY IMBALANCE*

Brain chemistry imbalances, or neurochemical disturbances, can have a profound effect on mental health. Neurochemicals are substances in the brain which control the communication between neurons and ultimately influence behavior, mood, and thought processes. When these chemicals are out of balance due to genetic factors or external influences such as stress, it can lead to psychiatric disorders such as depression, anxiety, and bipolar disorder.

The most common neurochemicals associated with mental health issues are serotonin, dopamine, and norepinephrine. Serotonin helps to regulate mood and contributes to feelings of well-being. When this chemical is out of balance, it can lead to depression or anxiety. Dopamine affects motivation and emotions, while an imbalance in this neurochemical may cause impulsivity or irritability. Lastly, norepinephrine plays a role in fear regulation and alertness; when there is too much or too little of this chemical present in the brain, it can trigger symptoms such as panic attacks or insomnia.

Hormones, like neurochemicals, play an important role in the brain's chemistry and mental health. Hormonal imbalances can lead to mood swings, irritability, depression, and even psychosis. The most notable hormones that are related to mental health are cortisol, estrogen, testosterone, and progesterone.

Cortisol is a stress hormone that helps regulate emotions and body functions in response to stressors. It is released during times of physical or emotional distress and plays a major role in the fight-or-flight reaction. Too much cortisol can result in depression or anxiety disorders due to its effect on serotonin levels.

Estrogen is important for female reproductive health but also has an effect on mood as it plays a role in serotonin regulation.

Higher levels of estrogen can cause feelings of happiness while lower levels often lead to sadness or irritability. Testosterone is important for male reproductive health but also affects mood by affecting dopamine levels; too much testosterone can lead to aggression while not enough can cause fatigue.

Progesterone helps regulate sleep cycles but it also helps keep cortisol levels balanced as well as control other hormones such as testosterone and estrogen. Low progesterone can lead to increased stress and depression whereas too much of this hormone could cause irritability or poor concentration skills.

These are just some examples of how these hormones have an effect on our mental health; there may be other hormones or factors at play that we don't yet fully understand. All these hormones interact with each other to create complex reactions that ultimately determine our overall emotional state and behavior patterns; thus, when any one of them is out of balance it can affect our mental health in profound ways.

Brain chemistry imbalance also refers to disruptions in the levels of neurotransmitters—chemical messengers that transmit signals in the brain. These neurotransmitters, such as serotonin, dopamine, and norepinephrine, play crucial roles in regulating mood, emotions, and cognitive functions. When the balance of these chemicals is disrupted, it can contribute to the development or exacerbation of mental health disorders.

For instance, an imbalance in serotonin levels is commonly associated with depression and anxiety. Low serotonin levels can lead to persistent feelings of sadness, anxiety, and a lack of interest in daily activities. Similarly, irregularities in dopamine levels are linked to conditions like schizophrenia and bipolar disorder. High dopamine levels can be associated with manic episodes and psychosis, while low levels may contribute to symptoms of depression.

Neurotransmitter imbalances can result from various factors, including genetic predisposition, environmental stressors, and medical conditions. For example, chronic stress can alter neurotransmitter systems, potentially leading to or worsening mental health issues. Additionally, certain medications, substance use, or hormonal changes can also impact brain chemistry.

Understanding and addressing brain chemistry imbalances is crucial in treating mental health disorders. Treatment strategies often involve medications that aim to restore neurotransmitter levels to a more balanced state. These medications, such as antidepressants or antipsychotics, work by either increasing or regulating the levels of specific neurotransmitters.

However, brain chemistry imbalance is just one aspect of mental health. It is essential to consider other factors, such as genetics, environment, and personal experiences, in a comprehensive approach to treatment and management. Addressing brain chemistry imbalances can significantly improve symptoms and overall well-being, but it often needs to be combined with other therapeutic approaches for optimal results.

❖ *NEUROLOGICAL CONDITIONS AND TRAUMATIC BRAIN INJURY*

Neurological conditions refer to any condition that affects the nervous system, including both physical and mental disorders. Both neurological conditions and traumatic brain injury can have significant impacts on a person's mental health, affecting their ability to function in day-to-day life as well as their overall sense of well-being.

Neurological conditions involve impairments or abnormalities in brain structure or function which can lead to symptoms such as mood changes, behavior problems, impaired cognition, and difficulty with activities of daily living. Common examples include Alzheimer's disease, multiple sclerosis (MS), Parkinson's disease, epilepsy, and traumatic brain injury (TBI). These conditions can have serious consequences for an individual's mental health, causing depression, anxiety, and other psychiatric disorders.

Alzheimer's disease is a progressive neurological disorder that results in memory loss and cognitive decline. As the disease progresses, individuals may experience difficulty with communication and decision-making due to impaired memory. This can lead to feelings of confusion, disorientation, and isolation which often result in significant psychological distress. In addition to these symptoms, those with Alzheimer's commonly suffer from depression or anxiety as they come to terms with their declining mental state.

Multiple sclerosis (MS) is another progressive neurological condition that can cause physical and mental health symptoms. Those with MS may experience difficulty with coordination, balance, and vision due to damage to the myelin sheaths which insulate nerve fibers in the central nervous system. Patients may also experience fatigue, depression, anxiety, and cognitive problems such as memory loss or impaired concentration.

Parkinson's disease is a neurodegenerative disorder that affects movement and cognition due to dopamine deficiency in the brain. Symptoms can include tremors, slowed movements, impaired speech, and writing abilities, as well as mood changes such as depression and anxiety. Depression is particularly common among those with Parkinson's disease; it is estimated that up to 50% of patients suffer from depression at some point during their illness.

Epilepsy is a disorder of the central nervous system characterized by recurrent seizures. It can cause physical and mental health symptoms such as confusion, anxiety, memory loss, depression, and impaired coordination. Seizures themselves may be accompanied by transient changes in behavior or cognitive function that can further complicate emotional well-being.

Traumatic brain injury (TBI) occurs when an individual suffers a blow to the head resulting in damage to their brain tissue. This type of injury often causes physical disability but it can also lead to psychological effects such as mood swings, irritability, aggression, impulse control problems, depression, anxiety, and sleep disturbances. TBI can also impact an individual's thinking abilities including their ability to concentrate and make decisions.

Stephen Hawking is arguably the most famous example of someone living with a neurological condition. Diagnosed with motor neuron disease, or ALS, at the age of 21, Professor Hawking experienced progressive physical disability and was eventually confined to a wheelchair. Despite this, he went on to become one of the greatest minds in modern physics and cosmology, dedicating himself to his research and writing extensively on his theories. Hawking's story is an inspiring example of how individuals can transcend even the most debilitating conditions through their own strength and determination.

Muhammad Ali is another well-known individual who suffered from a neurological condition. At age 42, Ali was diagnosed with Parkinson's disease due to boxing-related brain injuries sustained during his career. Despite the physical and mental struggles associated with his diagnosis, Ali remained active in public life, making appearances at various events and inspiring countless individuals around the world through his courage and grace.

Terry Sawchuk is a story of resilience and overcoming adversity. As one of the greatest goalies in NHL history, Sawchuk suffered many injuries throughout his career which eventually led to him being diagnosed with post-concussion syndrome. Despite his physical and mental health issues, he continued to play hockey until shortly before his death at the age of 40. He was inducted into the Hockey Hall of Fame in 1971 and remains an inspiration for many.

It is clear that neurological conditions and traumatic brain injury can have significant impacts on an individual's mental health. While the physical effects of these disorders are often more obvious, it is essential to remember that psychological symptoms can also be disabling and require treatment. Those suffering from a neurological condition or TBI should be encouraged to seek professional help in order to manage their symptoms and maintain their overall well-being. With proper care and support, individuals with these conditions can lead fulfilling lives despite any challenges they may face.

Neurological conditions and traumatic brain injury (TBI) both impact brain function but differ in their origins and effects.

Neurological conditions refer to a variety of disorders affecting the nervous system. These include:

Neurodegenerative Diseases: Diseases such as Alzheimer's and Parkinson's involve progressive damage to brain cells, leading to symptoms like memory loss, motor difficulties, and behavioral changes.

Epilepsy: This disorder causes recurrent seizures due to abnormal brain electrical activity, affecting consciousness and motor control.

Multiple Sclerosis (MS): An autoimmune condition where the immune system attacks nerve fibers' protective coverings, leading to symptoms like muscle weakness, coordination issues, and cognitive changes.

Migraine: A chronic headache condition characterized by severe, recurring headaches often accompanied by nausea, sensitivity to light, and other symptoms.

Traumatic brain injury (TBI) results from an external force damaging the brain, such as from accidents, falls, or violence. The severity of TBI ranges from mild, like concussions, to severe injuries with significant cognitive and physical impairments. Mild TBI might cause headaches and dizziness, while severe TBI can lead to prolonged unconsciousness, memory issues, and major behavioral changes.

Both neurological conditions and TBI require comprehensive treatment. Neurological conditions are managed with medications, physical therapy, and lifestyle changes aimed at symptom management and slowing progression. TBI treatment focuses on acute care and rehabilitation to address physical, cognitive, and emotional impacts. Managing these conditions typically involves a multidisciplinary approach to support recovery and improve quality of life.

2. PSYCHOLOGICAL FACTORS

Psychological factors play a significant role in influencing mental health, behavior, and emotional well-being. These factors encompass a range of internal processes, experiences, and traits that shape how individuals think, feel, and respond to life's challenges. Psychological factors can contribute to the development of mental health conditions or act as protective elements that promote resilience and emotional balance.

One key psychological factor is cognitive processes, which refer to how individuals perceive and interpret the world around them. Negative thought patterns, such as catastrophizing or irrational beliefs, can increase the risk of developing anxiety, depression, and other mental health issues. On the other hand, positive thinking and problem-solving skills can enhance emotional well-being and reduce vulnerability to stress.

Personality traits also have a strong influence on mental health. Certain traits, such as high neuroticism, can make individuals more prone to experiencing intense emotional responses, stress, and mood disorders. Conversely, traits like emotional stability and high levels of conscientiousness are often associated with better mental health outcomes.

Coping mechanisms are another essential psychological factor. How a person manages stress and adversity significantly impacts their mental health. Adaptive coping strategies, such as seeking social support, practicing mindfulness, or engaging in physical activity, can buffer against the effects of stress. In contrast, maladaptive coping strategies, like avoidance, substance use, or self-isolation, can exacerbate mental health challenges.

Past experiences, particularly early childhood experiences and trauma, can shape an individual's psychological makeup. Adverse childhood experiences (ACEs), such as abuse or neglect, increase the risk of developing mental health conditions later in life. Traumatic experiences can lead to conditions like post-traumatic stress disorder (PTSD) or contribute to anxiety and depression. However, positive experiences, such as supportive relationships and a nurturing environment, can foster resilience and emotional health.

Emotional regulation is another critical psychological factor. The ability to manage and express emotions in healthy ways can influence how individuals respond to stress and conflict. Difficulty regulating emotions can lead to impulsive behaviors, mood instability, and heightened vulnerability to mental health disorders such as borderline personality disorder or anxiety.

Self-esteem and self-concept also play a pivotal role. Low self-esteem can contribute to feelings of worthlessness, insecurity, and increased risk for depression and anxiety. A positive self-concept, where individuals feel confident in their abilities and sense of self, can promote mental wellness and resilience in the face of challenges.

Beliefs and attitudes about oneself and the world can profoundly affect mental health. Pessimistic or rigid beliefs may increase susceptibility to mental health disorders, whereas optimism and a growth mindset can enhance emotional well-being and foster adaptability in difficult situations.

Mind-related disorders caused by psychological factors can vary widely, but trauma, neglect, sexual abuse, physical abuse, and emotional abuse are some of the most common sources.

Trauma is the result of extreme or overwhelming experiences that overwhelm an individual's ability to cope with or manage the situation. The traumatic experience could be a single event, such

As a car accident or natural disaster; it could also involve chronic stressors such as living in an unsafe neighborhood or enduring long periods of isolation.

Neglect is a kind of psychological trauma. It happens when someone does not get the love and care they need, like children who do not get enough love and attention from their parents. This deprives them of the emotional support and security they need to develop into a healthy, confident individual.

Sexual abuse is another form of psychological trauma that can have devastating consequences. It includes rape, molestation, or any kind of sexual contact between an adult and a minor. This type of trauma is especially damaging because it often leads to feelings of guilt, shame, fear, and mistrust in relationships.

Oprah Winfrey has become an icon of resilience and empowerment, particularly as a woman of color in the media and entertainment industry. She was sexually molested by her cousin at nine years of age, and then again by an uncle and a family friend later on. Despite the trauma she experienced, Oprah managed to overcome it, even avoiding the manifestation of mental illnesses. Oprah also identified young girls who were sexually abused at a tender age, one of which was molested by her own father when she was four years old. This caused the girl to develop posttraumatic stress disorder (PTSD).

In order to set an example for other survivors of sexual abuse, Oprah has been vocal about her experience and raised awareness around this issue in multiple talk shows and interviews. Through her platform, she has been able to create a safe space for survivors to speak up without feeling ashamed or judged. In addition, Oprah has also provided intense support through different charities and organizations that focus on helping other victims of sexual violence.

Moreover, Oprah created O: The Oprah Magazine in 2000 as a means to further spread awareness regarding this issue while providing inspiration to those going through similar circumstances. In the magazine, Winfrey frequently addresses topics related to sexual assault such as ways in which victims can reclaim their power after experiencing trauma. She also speaks out about how society should take measures against abusive behavior and offers advice on how survivors can recover from such experiences with love and compassion.

Physical abuse involves inflicting physical harm on someone else in order to gain power and control over that person. Examples include hitting, slapping, choking, pushing down stairs, or throwing objects at someone. Physical abuse can cause physical injuries as well as lasting emotional scars such as depression, anxiety, and Post-Traumatic Stress Disorder (PTSD).

Emotional abuse includes verbal or emotional threats, insults, humiliation, shaming, and manipulation. It can be just as damaging as physical abuse and often leads to low self-esteem and feelings of worthlessness.

Prince Harry of Sussex has faced a lifelong battle with mental illness, beginning when he was just a boy. His beloved mother, Princess Diana, tragically passed away when he was only 12 years old. The overwhelming grief and loss Harry experienced as a result of her death triggered his mental illness, resulting in an outpouring of rage and panic attacks that would control his life for the next two decades.

In the years following his mother's death, reports began to circulate about Harry's increasingly reckless behavior. He had begun smoking and drinking heavily, often leading to wild brawls and other outbursts in public places. His mental health was steadily declining as he struggled to cope with his inner demons, overwhelmed by anxiety and depression.

After 20 long years of battling this illness, Prince Harry finally sought help from specialists in order to get his life back on track. Through therapy sessions and intensive self-reflection, he was able to channel the rage and anguish from his mother's passing into something positive – finding acceptance and healing from the deep emotional wounds inflicted over these two decades of struggle.

Prince Harry's story is proof that no one is invincible; we are all vulnerable to our own struggles regardless of how strong or successful we may appear on the surface. But with courage and determination, it's possible not just to survive but thrive despite our darkest moments – just like Prince Harry did against all odds.

A famous figure in the public eye has been an outspoken advocate for mental health awareness for many years. After facing a crisis in 2016, which led to their hospitalization due to a severe panic attack, she decided it was time for a change.

She sought help from professionals who diagnosed her with lupus and bipolar disorder — two illnesses that she has since spoken openly about in interviews and on social media. Following her diagnosis, she learned how to manage both illnesses through medication as well as therapy sessions and lifestyle changes such as reducing stress and getting more restful sleep.

Throughout her teenage years, the hate comments she received online from trolls and fans alike caused her to struggle with suicidal thoughts. But despite the obstacles, she has become increasingly vocal about mental health issues in order to spread awareness and erase the stigma surrounding them.

This famous figure encouraging people to embrace their emotional struggles as a part of life and deal with them in healthy ways is none other than Selena Gomez.

These types of experiences can have lasting negative impacts on an individual's mental health. Trauma can lead to symptoms such as depression and anxiety as well as more severe mental illnesses like post-traumatic stress disorder (PTSD). Neglect has been linked to various developmental delays including social and academic problems later in life. Sexual abuse victims often struggle with feelings of guilt and shame while physical abuse victims may suffer from low self-esteem and difficulty trusting others. Those who experience emotional abuse may become emotionally withdrawn and isolated due to fear or mistrust.

Overall, it is essential for those suffering from mind-related disorders caused by psychological factors such as trauma or neglect to understand that they are not alone in their struggles; there is help available if needed through professional counseling services as well as through self-care practices aimed at improving overall wellness holistically over time. With patience and the right support, those suffering from psychological trauma can learn how to manage their symptoms in order to live a happy and fulfilling life.

In summary, psychological factors are intricately linked to mental health and overall well-being. Cognitive patterns, personality traits, coping mechanisms, past experiences, emotional regulation, self-esteem, and personal beliefs all interact to influence an individual's mental health trajectory. Understanding these factors can help in developing targeted strategies for maintaining mental health and promoting resilience.

3. ENVIRONMENTAL FACTORS

Environmental factors refer to external influences that affect an individual's mental health, well-being, and behavior. These factors encompass a wide range of social, economic, and physical conditions that interact with psychological and biological aspects to shape mental health outcomes.

Social environment plays a crucial role in mental health. Supportive relationships with family, friends, and the community provide emotional backing, reducing stress and promoting well-being. Conversely, social isolation, poor family dynamics, or toxic relationships can lead to increased feelings of loneliness, anxiety, and depression. Social support acts as a protective factor, helping individuals navigate life's challenges, whereas a lack of support can exacerbate mental health problems.

Socioeconomic status is another significant environmental factor. Individuals living in poverty or facing financial instability are at a higher risk for mental health issues. The stress of meeting basic needs, such as housing, food, and healthcare, can increase vulnerability to depression, anxiety, and other mental disorders. In contrast, financial security often provides greater access to mental health resources and stability, promoting better mental health outcomes.

Work and school environments also greatly influence mental health. A positive, supportive work or academic environment can foster growth, confidence, and satisfaction. However, toxic workplaces, high levels of stress, bullying, or job insecurity can lead to burnout, anxiety, and depression. Work-life balance and job satisfaction play key roles in maintaining mental health.

Cultural and societal norms affect how mental health is perceived and addressed. In cultures or societies where mental health is stigmatized, individuals may be less likely to seek help, worsening their condition. On the other hand, environments where mental health is openly discussed and supported can encourage individuals to seek care and improve their well-being.

Physical environment also has a profound impact on mental health. Living conditions, such as overcrowding, exposure to violence, and unsafe neighborhoods, can contribute to chronic stress and anxiety. Natural disasters, climate change, and pollution can create additional stressors that influence mental well-being. Access to green spaces, clean air, and safe communities promotes relaxation, physical activity, and mental wellness.

Childhood environment is particularly influential in shaping mental health throughout life. Adverse childhood experiences (ACEs), such as abuse, neglect, or witnessing violence, increase the likelihood of developing mental health issues in adulthood. A stable and nurturing childhood environment, on the other hand, can foster emotional resilience and healthy psychological development.

Education and access to healthcare are vital environmental factors as well. Higher education levels often correlate with better mental health outcomes, partly due to increased knowledge of self-care and access to resources. Access to affordable healthcare, including mental health services, plays a crucial role in preventing and treating mental health disorders.

The environment we inhabit can also play a role in the development of mental illness. For example, living in poverty or an area with high levels of crime may put individuals at greater risk for developing depression and anxiety disorders due to the stress associated with these situations. Also, those who live in areas that lack access to adequate education and healthcare services are often more likely to experience poorer mental health outcomes due to limited resources available.

Substance abuse is another environmental factor that can lead to mental health problems. The use of drugs and alcohol has been linked to higher rates of suicide attempts as well as an increased risk of developing long-term psychiatric issues such as schizophrenia or bipolar disorder. Long-term substance abuse can lead to changes in brain function which can cause issues such as impaired decision-making and memory loss.

Social isolation is another environmental factor that can contribute to the development of mental illness. Those who are socially isolated often experience more loneliness and depression, due in part to a lack of support from family and friends. This type of environment often leads to an individual feeling unsupported or misunderstood, leading them to engage in negative coping mechanisms such as self-medication or avoidance of social situations. Additionally, those living with chronic illnesses may be at greater risk for developing psychological issues due to their decreased ability to participate in activities that bring joy or purpose into their lives.

Winter blues, or Seasonal Affective Disorder (SAD), is another environmental factor associated with mental health issues. Reduced exposure to sunlight during the colder months can cause changes in brain chemistry that lead to feelings of sadness, lethargy, and irritability. Fortunately, SAD is a treatable condition and there are many options available for those who suffer from this type of seasonal depression such as light therapy and vitamin D supplementation.

People living in areas affected by war or civil unrest often experience psychological trauma due to the violence and extreme circumstances they are exposed to. This trauma can lead to symptoms of Post-Traumatic Stress Disorder (PTSD), including flashbacks, nightmares, difficulty sleeping, hypervigilance, feelings of guilt or shame, and depression.

Those who live in poverty are also at an increased risk of developing mental health issues. Poverty often leads to an individual feeling helpless and hopeless due to their inability to meet even basic needs such as food or shelter. These feelings can lead to the development of depression and anxiety disorders which can be difficult to manage without proper support services.

Lack of access to nutritious food can also have lasting implications on an individual's mental health. Nutrient deficiencies due to a lack of access to a well-balanced diet can cause changes in brain chemistry that may trigger depression or other mood disorders. Additionally, those who live with food insecurity often experience higher levels of stress due to worries related to how they will provide enough food for themselves or their families each month. This chronic stress can take a toll on an individual's emotional well-being over time leading to higher rates of mental illness in these populations.

The Covid-19 pandemic has had a dramatic impact on mental health around the world, resulting in an increased risk of developing mental illness. The stress associated with living through a global pandemic, isolation from family and friends, and financial hardship due to job loss or reduced income have all been linked to higher levels of anxiety, depression, and other psychological issues.

The unprecedented nature of the pandemic has also caused many people to experience fear, uncertainty, and a heightened sense of vulnerability. These feelings can lead to feelings of helplessness and doom that can make it difficult for individuals to cope with their emotions. Additionally, lack of access to physical or mental health services due to restrictions imposed by governments around the world as well as preconceived notions about mental health can further exacerbate existing conditions or even lead to new ones.

The impact of Covid-19 on mental health goes beyond just adults; children are also being disproportionately affected. Studies have found that children who are socially isolated for long periods of time may be at greater risk for developing psychological issues such as anxiety, depression, or post-traumatic stress disorder (PTSD). This is particularly concerning in light of the fact that many schools have shifted to online learning this year which has further limited children's ability to engage with peers in positive ways.

Finally, there is evidence that the economic downturn brought on by Covid-19 has resulted in an increase in inequality which can lead to feelings of injustice or alienation among those who are most affected. This can further contribute to mental health struggles such as anxiety or depression since these individuals may struggle with feeling powerless over their circumstances.

Overall, it is important to recognize the various environmental factors that can lead to mental illnesses; this knowledge should be used to help advocate for policies and programs that can help individuals in need lead healthier, more fulfilling lives. It is also important to remember that everyone responds differently to different environmental factors, so it is essential to make sure that everyone has access to the resources necessary to provide support and promote mental health.

Understanding Epilepsy and Seizures

What is Epilepsy?

Epilepsy is a medical ailment that affects the brain and is categorized as a neurological disorder. In simple words, epilepsy indicates that there is something strange about how the brain operates. The brain is a sophisticated organ that governs everything we do, from moving our body to thinking and emotion. It communicates using electrical signals, much as how power runs through cables in our houses.

In a person with epilepsy, these electrical signals can become disorganized. This confusion leads to what we call seizures, which are brief bursts of electrical activity in the brain. These seizures might vary widely in how they manifest themselves. For other people, seizures could be relatively minor, involving little more than a moment of bewilderment. For others, seizures can be severe, resulting in intense shaking, loss of consciousness, and even injury.

Epilepsy may afflict anybody, regardless of age, gender, or origin. It is crucial to emphasize that having one seizure does not signify a person has epilepsy. A diagnosis of epilepsy is given only after a person has experienced two or more unprovoked seizures. Unprovoked means that the seizures occur without any evident reason, such as a high fever or a head injury.

There are many distinct forms of epilepsy, which can vary based on how seizures occur and where they begin in the brain. Some people may have only one form of seizure, while others may suffer numerous types throughout their lifetimes.

What is a Seizure?

A seizure is a breakdown of the brain's electrical circuitry. This problem can induce many symptoms, which can differ greatly from one individual to another. When a seizure happens, it interrupts normal brain activity and can lead to changes in behavior, movements, feelings, or awareness.

Seizures may be categorized into two primary categories: focal seizures and generalized seizures.

Focal seizures start in one single location of the brain. Depending on how these seizures occur, they can remain isolated to one location or spread to other sections of the brain. When a focal seizure lingers in one region, it may create limited symptoms, such as twitching in one hand or a weird sensation in one side of the body. Some persons may also notice changes in their emotions or sentiments during these seizures.

On the other hand, generalized seizures impact both sides of the brain from the very beginning. These seizures tend to be more obvious and might entail a loss of consciousness. There are various varieties of generalized seizures, but two of the most frequent are tonic-clonic seizures and absence seizures.

Tonic-clonic seizures, frequently referred to as grand mal seizures, are the most well-known form of seizure. During a tonic-clonic seizure, a person may first feel extremely rigid and lose consciousness (this is the tonic phase). Following this, the individual may begin to jerk and tremble violently (this is the clonic phase). These seizures can range from a few seconds to a few minutes, and thereafter, the person may feel very weary, disoriented, or even have a headache.

Absence seizures, previously known as petit mal seizures, are typically shorter and include momentary gaps in awareness. A person undergoing an absence seizure could stop what they are doing, look blankly, and not respond to anyone around them.

These episodes frequently last only a few seconds and may be misinterpreted for daydreaming, making them difficult to spot.

Understanding the distinction between epilepsy and seizures is crucial. While seizures can occur due to many reasons, such as a high temperature, a head injury, or withdrawal from narcotics, epilepsy is a long-term disorder defined by repeated, unprovoked seizures.

Famous People with Epilepsy

Recurrent seizures are a hallmark of epilepsy, a neurological illness that affects millions of individuals globally. Despite being common, the ailment still has a heavy stigma, which frequently results in misunderstandings and a lack of knowledge. Nonetheless, the experiences of people with epilepsy, particularly those who have attained professional success, provide light on the condition's reality. By telling their story, these people dispel misconceptions, raise awareness, and encourage others going through comparable struggles.

Rap legend Lil Wayne, who has made a name for himself in the music business, is one of the people who has courageously shared their experiences with epilepsy. He had epilepsy as a toddler and was born Dwayne Michael Carter Jr. This condition has significantly impacted his life and profession, and he has not held back when talking about the difficulties it brings. Lil Wayne has discussed how his epilepsy has impacted his everyday life and performances in a number of interviews. He talked about times when seizures interfered with his job and caused issues during recording sessions or live performances. Lil Wayne has persevered in his career in spite of these obstacles, utilizing his position to spread knowledge about epilepsy and show that having a chronic illness does not prevent one from succeeding.

Lil Wayne's open talks about his epilepsy are especially important because of the culture in which he lives. Hip-hop frequently places a strong emphasis on toughness and resilience, which can occasionally minimize vulnerability or health issues. Lil Wayne defies this stereotype by candidly addressing his illness, providing a more complex perspective on what it means to be a great artist who is also dealing with health concerns. Numerous teenage admirers who could be facing health issues find inspiration in his candor, which motivates them to speak up and get help rather than endure their suffering in secret.

Prince is another well-known musician who has struggled with epilepsy. The mysterious musician, who made revolutionary contributions to music, had epilepsy when he was a young boy. Prince overcame this serious health issue to create a renowned career that is defined by his inventive sound and thrilling live performances. In addition to being challenges to conquer, his experiences with epilepsy were deeply entwined with his artistic story.

Prince's struggles with epilepsy occasionally interfered with his performance, but he refused to let it overshadow his extraordinary skill. He frequently discussed how he managed the illness in interviews, emphasizing his will to overcome the constraints it placed on him. Prince's fortitude in the face of hardship served as a source of inspiration for many, demonstrating that skill, imagination, and willpower can overcome physical issues. He served as an example to other artists as well as to anybody facing their struggles, reaffirming that having epilepsy does not define a person's ability or restrict their chances of success.

The well-known actor and campaigner Danny Glover has also been candid about his battles with epilepsy. Throughout his decades-long career, Glover has utilized his position to promote social justice and health awareness, particularly with regard to epilepsy. He has openly discussed his own experiences with seizures, highlighting the significance of being aware of and comprehending the disease. Glover has stated unequivocally his belief in the need for assistance for those with epilepsy and the need to promote a greater awareness of the condition among the general public.

Glover has brought attention to the need for a greater understanding of epilepsy and the stigma that frequently surrounds it through his advocacy activities. By telling his personal story, he promotes understanding and a feeling of community among people impacted by the illness by inspiring others to talk about their experiences and get assistance. Glover's impact goes beyond the entertainment sector; his dedication to advocacy strikes a chord with many, demonstrating the critical role prominent personalities can play in changing attitudes and fostering a more accepting atmosphere for people with epilepsy.

Known for her well-received parts in television dramas like "ER" and "The Good Wife," Julianna Margulies is another well-known person who has publicly talked about her experiences with seizures. Although Margulies has always enthralled audiences with her performances, her open conversations about her condition have had a profound effect. She has underlined the need to have a solid support network for those with epilepsy, emphasizing that without the appropriate tools and knowledge, the journey may be overwhelming.

Margulies has pushed for greater knowledge and instruction regarding epilepsy, emphasizing the value of discussing the illness with others. She hopes that by sharing her experience, she will inspire others who might be going through difficult times in silence to get treatment and realize they are not alone. Being a well-known actress gives her the ability to reach a large audience, which she utilizes to raise awareness of the difficulties related to epilepsy and promote a better understanding of the condition.

Considered by many to be one of the best tennis players of all time, Serena Williams has also experienced health issues, such as seizures. Williams has frequently discussed the value of putting one's health and wellbeing first, especially in high-performance sports. Her candor about her health issues highlights the difficulties of managing a medical condition while striving for success in a challenging profession.

Williams has stated unequivocally that success on and off the court depends on recognizing health concerns. Her openness about her experiences inspires people to take control of their health and get help when needed. By sharing her experience, Williams demonstrates that success is not without its difficulties and contributes to normalizing conversations about epilepsy and other health issues. She is a role model for many and encourages others to fight for their health and wellbeing. Therefore, her impact goes beyond athletics.

The well-known actor Samuel L. Jackson, who has a multi-decade career, has also talked about his experiences with epilepsy. Jackson's openness about his illness has been crucial in increasing public understanding of epilepsy and its associated difficulties. He has talked candidly about how seizures have affected his life and career, highlighting the significance of raising awareness and educating people about the condition.

Jackson's impact goes beyond the movie industry; his readiness to talk about his health issues promotes an accepting and understanding society. By speaking up, he inspires people to get treatment and face their health issues head-on. His advocacy work aims to increase awareness and support for those with epilepsy, and his experience emphasizes the need to acknowledge the illness as a real health problem.

It's interesting to note that fictional characters have also portrayed epilepsy in a variety of stories; thus, the ailment is not just represented by real people. Rudolf Erich Raspe's character Baron von Munchausen is a prominent example. The Baron has been shown as suffering from a variety of illnesses, including epilepsy, in different versions of his stories. This portrayal demonstrates how epilepsy has influenced narrative and literature, indicating its enduring existence in human society.

Fictional depictions of the disorder can greatly influence public impressions of epilepsy. By humanizing people with epilepsy and highlighting their resiliency, storytellers help to advance a wider knowledge of the condition by incorporating characters with epilepsy into their works. These stories frequently work to dispel prejudices and compel viewers to sympathize with those who are dealing with health issues.

It has also been hypothesized that historical personalities like Napoleon Bonaparte suffered from epilepsy. Various sources indicate that the French military leader could have experienced seizures. However, historical material from that period is not totally solid. This demonstrates the fact that epilepsy is not a recent development; rather, it has existed for ages.

Napoleon's tale serves as a reminder that many significant figures in history have struggled with their health. Gaining knowledge from these historical narratives helps one to comprehend how epilepsy has been seen and understood across time, as well as how it has affected those in positions of authority.

One cannot stress the significance of increasing awareness and decreasing stigma as discussions regarding epilepsy continue to change. The hardships and difficulties of the illness are illustrated by the stories of people such as Lil Wayne, Prince, Danny Glover, Julianna Margulies, Serena Williams, and Samuel L. Jackson. Because of their activism and candor, they greatly advance the conversation on epilepsy and promote societal acceptance and understanding.

Whether told from the experiences of actual people or made-up characters, the power of storytelling is still essential for dismantling obstacles and creating a more accepting society for people with epilepsy. By inspiring and empowering others, these leaders' talks start a chain reaction that promotes more awareness and support for those who are affected by the illness.

To sum up, the experiences of these well-known people shed light on the difficulties of having epilepsy. Their stories are a reminder that people can overcome health issues with fortitude and resiliency and that excellence is possible even in the face of adversity. They open the door for more knowledge and acceptance via their advocacy, which eventually helps create a society that is more sympathetic and accepting of people with epilepsy. In addition to giving people hope, their stories highlight how crucial it is to help one another on the path to improved health and wellbeing.

Living with Epilepsy

Living with epilepsy can be tough, but many people discover methods to manage their condition efficiently. Each person's experience with epilepsy is unique, and the consequences of the illness can vary greatly. However, some different therapeutic choices and tactics can help individuals lead satisfying lives despite their obstacles.

Medication is one of the most popular ways of treatment for epilepsy. There are many different types of drugs available, and doctors work carefully with patients to identify the exact one or combination that effectively manages their seizures. Patients with epilepsy need to take their medications as recommended since this can dramatically lessen the frequency and severity of seizures. Skipping doses or quitting medicine without contacting a doctor might lead to increased seizures and problems.

In addition to medicine, patients with epilepsy might benefit by recognizing and avoiding seizure triggers. Triggers can vary considerably from person to person and may include things such as stress, lack of sleep, specific meals, or flashing lights. By knowing what causes their seizures, individuals can take proactive actions to decrease their exposure to these circumstances. Keeping a notebook to chronicle seizures and any suspected causes might help individuals and their healthcare professionals create effective management techniques.

Support networks play a significant role in helping persons with epilepsy navigate their disease. Having a strong support system of family, friends, and healthcare professionals may give emotional and practical aid. Support groups, either in-person or online, can give a sense of camaraderie and understanding for individuals living with epilepsy. Sharing experiences with others who encounter similar issues may be inspiring and reassuring.

Education is another crucial component of living with epilepsy. Understanding the disease, its symptoms, and treatment choices may empower individuals and their families. Learning about seizures and how to respond during an episode may be useful for everyone concerned. For example, understanding how to keep a person safe during a seizure, such as moving things out of the way and laying them on their side, can assist prevent injuries.

In addition to medical therapy and support, lifestyle modifications can also play a crucial role in treating epilepsy. Maintaining a healthy lifestyle can help with general well-being and lessen the frequency of seizures. Regular exercise, a balanced diet, and proper sleep hygiene can significantly improve a person's health and help lower stress levels.

Stress management approaches, such as mindfulness, meditation, and relaxation exercises, can be particularly effective for those with epilepsy. Finding efficient techniques to cope with stress can help prevent seizures that may be induced by worry or tension. Engaging in things they enjoy, such as hobbies, art, or spending time with loved ones, may help enhance their mental health and reduce stress.

In certain circumstances, when drugs do not adequately control seizures, additional therapeutic options may be investigated. These choices can include dietary therapy, such as the ketogenic diet, which is high in fats and low in carbs and has been demonstrated to assist some patients with epilepsy. Additionally, some individuals may benefit from therapies like vagus nerve stimulation (VNS) or even surgery, depending on their condition and the type of epilepsy they have.

While living with epilepsy can be tough, many people have discovered ways to embrace life completely. Stories of individuals who have surmounted hurdles due to their disease serve as a reminder that epilepsy does not determine a person's potential. With adequate treatment, support, and a positive mentality, persons with epilepsy may follow their aspirations and enjoy successful lives.

CONSEQUENCES OF A DENIAL

No matter the individual or their circumstances, denying mental health needs can have serious consequences for both physical and emotional well-being. When an individual is in denial about their mental health condition, they are unable to seek out proper treatment which could help them manage their symptoms and improve their overall quality of life.

The most immediate consequence of denying mental health needs is increased stress and anxiety levels due to avoidance of the issue. By avoiding seeking professional support, individuals may experience a heightened state of psychological distress on a more frequent basis than if they had addressed the issue head-on. This could lead to more severe symptoms such as panic attacks, insomnia, or even depression. In addition to this, chronic stress has been linked to physical ailments such as headaches, chronic pain, and even heart disease.

Denial of mental health needs can also lead to an inability to effectively manage daily responsibilities due to the overwhelming feelings associated with such avoidance tactics. This could further hamper an individual's ability to perform at their job or school as well as maintain relationships. In addition, when individuals are in denial about their mental health condition it is much more difficult for them to recognize warning signs when symptoms become too severe and require professional intervention. This can lead to more frequent hospitalizations or other serious consequences such as suicide attempts.

Finally, denying mental health needs can lead to a cycle of self-defeating behaviors that perpetuate the original problem. Individuals may find themselves engaging in unhealthy coping mechanisms such as substance abuse, self-harm, or disordered eating in order to cope with the intense emotions they are feeling. This can contribute to even more serious mental health problems and further prevent them from getting the help they need.

The consequences of denial, especially when it comes to mental health or life challenges, can be profound and far-reaching. Denial is a defense mechanism where an individual refuses to acknowledge a problem or situation, often as a way of avoiding emotional distress. While it might provide temporary relief, long-term denial can have detrimental effects on an individual's well-being and relationships.

One major consequence of denial is delayed treatment or intervention. In the context of mental health, refusing to acknowledge symptoms of depression, anxiety, or other disorders can prevent individuals from seeking professional help. This delay often leads to worsening symptoms, making the condition more difficult to manage or treat. The earlier mental health issues are addressed, the better the outcomes; denial can significantly hinder this process, causing the problem to become more entrenched.

Denial can also lead to deterioration of relationships. Refusing to acknowledge a personal issue, such as substance abuse or emotional instability, can strain relationships with family, friends, and partners. Loved ones may feel helpless or frustrated when attempts to address the problem are met with resistance or dismissal. Over time, denial can create a barrier to communication and trust, isolating the individual further.

Another consequence is the escalation of stress and emotional pain. By avoiding the underlying issue, individuals in denial often experience mounting internal tension. Suppressed emotions or unresolved problems can manifest as increased anxiety, irritability, or even physical symptoms like headaches, fatigue, or digestive issues. Denial doesn't eliminate the problem; it merely pushes it out of conscious awareness, where it can continue to affect emotional and physical health.

Denial can also lead to risky behaviors. In some cases, individuals may engage in harmful behaviors, such as substance abuse, reckless spending, or unhealthy coping mechanisms, in an effort to maintain the illusion that everything is under control. These behaviors can exacerbate the original issue, creating a cycle of avoidance and negative consequences.

In more extreme cases, denial can result in legal or financial problems. For instance, denying the severity of an addiction or refusing to recognize irresponsible financial habits can lead to serious consequences, such as loss of employment, bankruptcy, or legal issues. Refusing to confront these realities often leads to more severe outcomes than if they were addressed early on.

Furthermore, denial can contribute to poor decision-making. When individuals fail to acknowledge the full scope of a situation, they may make choices that are misinformed or based on incomplete understanding. This can lead to decisions that further complicate or worsen the situation, whether in their personal life, career, or health.

In summary, denial might offer short-term relief from emotional discomfort, but its long-term consequences can be severe. From delayed treatment and strained relationships to emotional distress and risky behaviors, denial can deepen the very problems it seeks to avoid. Acknowledging and addressing the issue, though challenging, is often the first step toward healing and positive change.

MANAGEMENT OF MENTAL ILLNESSES

Once you have a precise diagnosis that accurately reflects the mental health issues that you are currently dealing with, it is important to begin managing these illnesses. This can be difficult to do, but with the right support and guidance from knowledgeable professionals and peers, it is possible.

When managing mental illnesses, there are several steps that should be taken in order to ensure success. The first step is education about the illness itself, its symptoms, and its treatments. It is essential for individuals struggling with mental health issues to understand their condition as well as potential treatment options so they can make informed decisions about their own well-being. Additionally, familiarizing yourself with other supportive resources such as peer groups and online communities can provide invaluable assistance during times of distress or crisis.

The second step is to develop an individualized plan for managing your mental health. This may include regular counseling, medication management, and lifestyle changes such as healthy eating habits, exercise, stress reduction techniques, and increased social support. During this process, it is important to identify goals that are realistic and meaningful to you in order to help guide the process of recovery.

Finally, the third step is engaging in consistent self-care. Self-care can be anything from taking a hot bath or going for a walk to simply listening to music or reading a book. Whatever it is that makes you feel nurtured and relaxed should become part of your daily routine so that you can continue on the path toward healing. Additionally, monitoring moods, behaviors, and changes in thinking can provide insight into how the management of your mental health is progressing.

1. PSYCHOLOGICAL THERAPY

Psychological therapy is an integral part of mental health management and can be a powerful tool for helping individuals to gain insight into their current situation, develop coping strategies, and work toward personal healing. Common forms of psychological therapy include cognitive behavioral therapy (CBT), interpersonal psychotherapy (IPT), dialectical behavior therapy (DBT), and psychodynamic psychotherapy.

Cognitive-behavioral therapy helps people change how they think about themselves, the world around them, and their behaviors. This type of therapy focuses on identifying patterns in thinking that are unhelpful or inaccurate, challenging these distorted thoughts with evidence from reality, and replacing them with more adaptive thought patterns. Through this process of identifying negative beliefs and replacing them with more positive ones, individuals can learn to better manage their symptoms and gain a more balanced outlook on life.

Interpersonal psychotherapy (IPT) is another type of therapy that focuses on the relationships an individual has with others as well as how they interact in social situations. IPT often involves exploring past experiences and current circumstances in order to gain insight into troubling interpersonal patterns. By doing so, individuals can work towards improving communication skills, developing healthier boundaries within relationships, and ultimately gaining greater satisfaction from social interactions.

Dialectical behavior therapy (DBT) is another psychological treatment approach that helps people learn new ways of responding to difficult emotions without resorting to destructive behaviors such as self-harm or substance abuse. DBT emphasizes both acceptance and change, helping people gain insight into their behaviors and providing them with skills for managing distress.

Finally, psychodynamic psychotherapy is a form of therapy that focuses on understanding the deeper psychological processes behind an individual's behavior by exploring past experiences. This type of therapy helps individuals to uncover unconscious conflicts or trauma that may be causing emotional pain and distress in their lives. By coming to terms with these difficult memories, individuals can learn to better manage current challenges and move forward in life.

One of the major benefits of psychological therapy is that it helps individuals become more aware of themselves on both an interpersonal and intrapersonal level. Through talking about experiences or feelings within a safe space, people can gain a greater understanding of their own thoughts, beliefs, values, and behaviors. This understanding can help to increase self-awareness, which in turn can support mental health management.

Psychological therapy also serves as a platform for change. By exploring negative or unhelpful thought patterns and developing healthier ways of or behaving, individuals can learn new skills and strategies for managing difficult emotions and situations in life. This process of re-framing beliefs and replacing them with more constructive ones can help to foster greater emotional resilience, enabling people to cope more effectively with stressors life throws their way.

Finally, psychological therapy provides emotional support and validation. Working with a mental health professional who is trained in understanding human psychology and behavior can be incredibly healing for individuals struggling to understand their own experiences. Talking through problems and feelings with someone who has knowledge of the subject matter can help to alleviate emotional distress, providing comfort during difficult times.

2. MEDICATIONS

Medication can also be an important part of mental health management and can be used to supplement psychological therapy or on its own. There are two main types of medication that are used to treat mental health disorders: psychopharmacological medications and psychiatric drugs.

Psychopharmacological medications, such as antidepressants and antianxiety medications, work by targeting specific brain chemicals in order to reduce symptoms associated with a particular disorder. These medications help to alter the levels of neurotransmitters (chemicals) in the brain which can then improve mood, decrease feelings of anxiety, or reduce other symptoms related to mental illness. However, it's important to note that these medications may take several weeks before their full effects are felt, so caution must be taken when deciding to start a course of medication.

Psychiatric drugs, such as antipsychotics, work by directly targeting brain receptors in order to reduce symptoms associated with mental health disorders. Unlike psychopharmacological medications, psychiatric drugs can take effect more quickly and are typically used for managing more severe forms of mental illness. These medications help to improve cognitive functioning and stabilize moods, allowing individuals to better manage their symptoms and lead more productive lives.

Other forms of medication, such as benzodiazepines, can also be used to treat mental health disorders in certain cases. These medications are often prescribed for short-term relief and work by calming the nervous system and reducing feelings of anxiety or panic. However, due to their potential for dependency and abuse, they must be taken with caution and under a doctor's supervision.

Medication is often prescribed alongside psychological therapy or self-help strategies in order to maximize its effectiveness; however, it's important to note that medication alone may not fully address the underlying causes of a disorder. In addition, certain medications come with side effects that may be uncomfortable or disruptive, so it's important to work closely with your doctor in order to find the right balance.

3. LIFESTYLE CHANGES AND SUPPORT NETWORKS

Engaging in relaxation activities and exercise is an important part of achieving mental health. Relaxation activities, such as yoga, tai chi, and meditation, are beneficial for relieving stress, calming the mind and body, and creating greater inner peace. Exercise also has numerous benefits for mental health. Studies have found that getting regular exercise can boost mood, increase energy levels, reduce feelings of anxiety or depression, and even help to improve cognitive functioning.

Exercise also releases endorphins which act as natural painkillers that can reduce physical tension and stress.

In addition to relaxation activities and exercise, it's important to incorporate healthy lifestyle habits into your daily routine in order to maintain good mental health. This includes getting enough sleep each night, eating a balanced diet with plenty of fruits and vegetables, avoiding excessive alcohol consumption or drug use, limiting caffeine intake if necessary, practicing mindful breathing throughout the day, engaging in regular leisure activities such as reading or listening to music; making time for social connections; setting realistic goals; taking breaks from work when necessary; practicing gratitude; expressing emotions through art or writing; spending time in nature; keeping a journal; seeking professional help if needed; identifying triggers that cause distress; managing finances responsibly; setting boundaries with others; asking for assistance when needed; challenging negative thought patterns with positive ones.

There is also great power in connecting with other people who understand your experience because no one should have to go through tough times alone. Through social connections with friends or family members, we can gain emotional support from those who care about us the most. Support groups are another great way of finding comfort during difficult times by talking with people who share similar experiences or struggles in life. There are also online support groups available where individuals around the world can connect with each other virtually about various topics related to mental health.

By committing yourself to relaxation activities and exercise on a regular basis while also incorporating healthy lifestyle habits into your daily routine you will be able to create a better balance between mind and body. When combined with psychological therapy or medication if necessary you will be armed with all the tools needed to manage your symptoms more effectively while still maintaining self-care at the same time.

A life filled with struggles and pain, yet one that shines brightly like a beacon of hope. A man who has endured mental health issues for most of his adult life, but still found the strength to excel in his chosen career. From actor to writer, comedian to television presenter, he has been a shining example of how overcoming adversity can lead to great success.

He's spoken openly about his battles with depression and bipolar disorder, how therapy and exercise have been essential in helping him stay on top of his mental health, and how taking medication prescribed by a doctor is an important part of his daily routine.

This man who has weathered so many storms with such grace and fortitude is none other than Stephen Fry. A true testament to the power of resilience and determination to overcome even the toughest of challenges.

In conclusion, mental health is an important aspect of our lives, and assessing it accurately helps us to manage our feelings and maintain a healthy lifestyle. Taking the time to get a precise diagnosis from a professional can make all the difference in terms of understanding your own mental health needs, as well as learning how best to meet them.

Additionally, it's also essential to recognize that this assessment process is ongoing - we must continue to assess ourselves regularly and adjust accordingly to any changes that may occur in our life circumstances or environment. With the right knowledge and attitude, we can take great strides toward improving our overall mental health. This chapter has provided valuable insight into how to go about taking this step toward bettering yourself.

Social support is a vital aspect of managing mental illnesses. Maintaining strong relationships with family, friends, or support groups provides emotional backing, reduces isolation, and encourages individuals to stay engaged in their treatment. Peer support, in particular, can offer a sense of understanding and shared experience, making the recovery process more bearable.

Ongoing monitoring and adjustments to treatment are essential, as mental health conditions can fluctuate over time. Regular check-ins with healthcare professionals help ensure that the treatment plan remains effective and that any necessary changes are made. In some cases, a combination of treatments, such as integrating medication adjustments with new therapeutic techniques, may be required to achieve better outcomes.

Managing mental illness is often a long-term process that involves continued effort and collaboration between the individual, healthcare providers, and their support system. With the right combination of medical, psychological, and social interventions, individuals can manage symptoms effectively, improve their quality of life, and work toward lasting recovery.

CHAPTER 3
ATTENTION DEFICIT HYPERACTIVITY DISORDER (ADHD)

Attention Deficit Hyperactivity Disorder (ADHD) is a mental disorder and neurological condition that affects the ability to focus, concentrate and manage one's energy level. People with ADHD typically exhibit difficulty paying attention, restlessness, and impulsiveness. It is often diagnosed in childhood but can persist into adulthood as well.

CAUSES OF ADHD

Scientific research is ongoing in an effort to better understand the causes of ADHD. Genetics are thought to play an important role, as studies have revealed specific genetic variations that may increase a person's risk for developing ADHD. Other potential causes and risk factors being explored include brain injury, environmental exposures during pregnancy or at a young age, alcohol and tobacco use during pregnancy, premature delivery, and low birth weight.

Furthermore, it has been found that children who have suffered from a traumatic event such as abuse or neglect do not show higher rates of ADHD than those without such experiences. This suggests that even though stress can be associated with mental health issues, it is unlikely to be the primary cause of ADHD.

Environmental factors might also play a part. For instance, contaminants such as lead or exposure to certain chemicals in the environment could increase a person's risk of developing ADHD. Additionally, research has suggested that there may be an association between having ADHD and exposure to second-hand smoke during childhood. However, more studies are needed to better understand how environmental factors may contribute to the development of ADHD.

Finally, some researchers believe that diet is related to the development of ADHD. Studies have shown that diets high in processed foods and sugar can increase hyperactivity levels in children with ADHD. While this indicates an association between diet and symptoms, further research into its role in ADHD is necessary.

TYPES OF ADHD

There are three main types of Attention Deficit Hyperactivity Disorder (ADHD): Predominantly Inattentive Presentation, Predominantly Hyperactive-Impulsive Presentation, and Combined Presentation.

1. PREDOMINANTLY INATTENTIVE PRESENTATION

Predominantly Inattentive Presentation, often referred to as ADHD-PI, is one of the three primary subtypes of Attention-Deficit/Hyperactivity Disorder (ADHD). This subtype is characterized primarily by difficulties sustaining attention, a tendency to become easily distracted, and a general lack of focus. Individuals with Predominantly Inattentive Presentation exhibit a unique set of symptoms that distinguish them from the other subtypes of ADHD.

One of the hallmark features of ADHD-PI is the persistent difficulty in maintaining attention, particularly on tasks or activities that require sustained mental effort. These individuals often need help concentrating on assignments, work-related projects, or leisure activities. As a result, they may frequently make careless mistakes, miss important details, or need help to complete tasks within the expected timeframe. This can lead to frustration and reduced academic, professional, and personal performance.

Moreover, individuals with ADHD-PI often report boredom or a lack of interest in tasks that do not capture their immediate attention. They may find it hard to engage with activities that are not inherently stimulating, making routine or monotonous tasks particularly challenging.

Forgetfulness is another common symptom of Predominantly Inattentive Presentation. These individuals may frequently misplace items, overlook appointments, and need help remembering important dates or deadlines. This forgetfulness can have significant consequences in their daily lives, affecting their relationships and responsibilities.

Easily becoming distracted is a characteristic trait of ADHD-PI. Even with external distractions, individuals with this subtype may find their minds wandering, making focusing on a single task easier. This constant internal distraction can interfere with their ability to complete tasks efficiently.

Those with Predominantly Inattentive Presentations may appear overly quiet and avoid engaging in conversations or social interactions. They may have difficulty following conversations, leading to feelings of isolation or social withdrawal. These challenges in communication and engagement can affect their relationships and hinder their ability to connect with others.

It's important to note that ADHD-PI can affect individuals of all ages, from children to adults. Early diagnosis and intervention are crucial to help individuals manage their symptoms effectively. Treatment options often include behavioural therapy, medication, and educational support tailored to the individual's needs.

Predominantly Inattentive Presentation is a subtype of ADHD characterized by difficulties sustaining attention, boredom or disinterest, forgetfulness, and a propensity to become easily distracted. Recognizing these symptoms is essential for early intervention and support to help individuals with ADHD-PI lead fulfilling lives and achieve their potential.

2. PREDOMINANTLY HYPERACTIVE - IMPULSIVE PRESENTATION

Predominantly Hyperactive-Impulsive Presentation is another distinct subtype of AttentionDeficit/Hyperactivity Disorder (ADHD). As the name suggests, this presentation primarily manifests through symptoms related to hyperactivity and impulsivity, setting it apart from the other subtypes of ADHD.

One prominent feature of this ADHD subtype is impulsiveness. Individuals with Predominantly Hyperactive-Impulsive Presentations often struggle to exercise impulse control, leading to impulsive decision-making. They may act on immediate desires or urges without adequately considering the consequences. This impulsivity can have repercussions in their lives, from impulsive spending to risky behaviour.

Interrupting others during conversations and excessive talking are common behavioural traits of this subtype. These individuals may find waiting their turn during discussions challenging, frequently interjecting or finishing others' sentences. Their excessive talking can be seen as a way to release their inner restlessness or a manifestation of their racing thoughts.

In addition to impulsivity and excessive talking, individuals with Predominantly HyperactiveImpulsive Presentation often struggle with maintaining stillness. They may constantly fidget, tap their feet, or move around, even when it is expected to sit quietly. This restlessness can be disruptive in academic or professional settings and make it challenging to engage in activities requiring prolonged sitting periods.

Furthermore, people with this type of ADHD often have a shorter attention span, making it difficult to focus on tasks or activities. They may become easily distracted by external stimuli or racing thoughts, impeding their productivity and task completion.

These individuals may also find it difficult to sit still for extended periods. The urge to move or fidget may become overwhelming, making staying seated in a classroom, workplace, or social setting challenging. This can lead to difficulties adhering to societal norms and expectations, potentially affecting their relationships and academic or professional progress.

It's important to note that the Predominantly Hyperactive-Impulsive Presentation of ADHD is not limited to children. Adults can also exhibit these symptoms, impacting their daily lives and relationships.

Treatment for this ADHD subtype often involves a combination of behavioural therapies, counselling, and, in some cases, medication. Behavioural interventions help individuals develop impulse control, manage hyperactivity, and improve focus and attention.

3. COMBINED PRESENTATION

The Combined Presentation of Attention-Deficit/Hyperactivity Disorder (ADHD) is a subtype that combines symptoms from the Predominantly Inattentive Presentation and the

Predominantly Hyperactive-Impulsive Presentation. Individuals with this subtype exhibit a wide range of ADHD symptoms, making it one of the disorder's most complex and challenging forms.

One of the hallmark features of the Combined Presentation is the presence of inattentive symptoms. This means that individuals with this subtype struggle with maintaining focus and attention, leading to difficulties in tasks requiring sustained mental effort. They may have trouble organizing their thoughts, managing time, and completing tasks, similar to those with Predominantly Inattentive Presentations.

Individuals with the Combined Presentation also experience hyperactive-impulsive symptoms.

This includes restlessness, impulsivity, and difficulty maintaining stillness, characteristic of the Predominantly Hyperactive-Impulsive Presentation. These individuals may fidget, talk excessively, interrupt conversations, and act impulsively without considering the consequences of their actions.

The combination of inattentive and hyperactive-impulsive symptoms in the Combined Presentation can create a complex and often challenging set of behaviours. Individuals may struggle in various aspects of their lives, including academics, work, relationships, and social interactions. Their impulsiveness may lead to impulsive decision-making, which can have significant consequences.

Moreover, some individuals with the Combined Presentation may also exhibit aggressive behaviour. This aggression can be a result of frustration and difficulty managing their symptoms. They may become easily overwhelmed by their inability to control their impulses and focus their attention, leading to outbursts of anger or irritability.

Managing ADHD with the Combined Presentation typically requires a comprehensive and multifaceted approach. Treatment may include behavioural therapy, counselling, medication, and educational support. The goal is to help individuals with this subtype develop strategies to manage their inattentive and hyperactive-impulsive symptoms and address any associated emotional and behavioural challenges.

It's essential for individuals with the Combined Presentation, as well as their families and support networks, to understand the nature of this subtype and seek appropriate interventions. With the right support and treatment, individuals with ADHD Combined Presentation can learn to manage their symptoms effectively and lead fulfilling lives, achieving their full potential despite their unique challenges.

Although there are three main types of ADHD, it is important to note that every individual's experience will be unique as many people do not fit neatly into one single category. It is therefore crucial to seek an accurate diagnosis from a medical professional so that the best available treatment options can be identified.

SIGNS AND SYMPTOMS

Attention-Deficit/Hyperactivity Disorder (ADHD) is a neurodevelopmental condition that affects millions of individuals worldwide, with symptoms typically appearing in childhood and often persisting into adulthood. While the presentation of ADHD can vary significantly from person to person, some common signs and symptoms provide insight into the nature of this complex disorder.

- **DIFFICULTY PAYING ATTENTION OR FOCUSING ON TASKS:**

One of the hallmark features of ADHD is an ongoing struggle with maintaining attention and focus. Individuals with ADHD often find it challenging to concentrate on tasks or activities requiring prolonged mental effort. They may become easily distracted by extraneous stimuli, even in relatively quiet environments. This difficulty in paying attention can manifest in various aspects of their lives, from school and work to everyday tasks and conversations.

- **MAKING DECISIONS WITHOUT CONSIDERING CONSEQUENCES:**

Impulsivity is another prominent symptom of ADHD. Individuals with ADHD may act on immediate impulses or desires without thoroughly considering the potential consequences of their actions. This impulsivity can lead to impulsive decision-making in personal and professional settings, which may have negative repercussions. Impulsivity can also manifest as difficulty waiting one's turn during conversations or interrupting others, disrupting communication and relationships.

- **RESTLESSNESS AND HYPERACTIVITY:**

Restlessness and hyperactivity are classic characteristics of ADHD, particularly in the Predominantly Hyperactive-Impulsive Presentation subtype. These individuals may constantly fidget, tap their feet, or move around, even when it is expected to sit quietly. This restlessness can make it difficult to stay focused during tasks or engage in activities requiring sustained stillness. In children, this hyperactivity often presents as climbing on furniture or running inappropriately, while in adults, it may manifest as an internal sense of restlessness.

- **DISORGANIZATION AND DIFFICULTY COMPLETING TASKS:**

Disorganization is a common challenge for individuals with ADHD. They may need help managing their belongings, keeping track of important documents, or maintaining an organized workspace. This disorganization extends to task completion as well. Individuals with ADHD often find it difficult to complete tasks promptly and efficiently, leading to frustration and inefficiency in their daily lives.

- **POOR TIME MANAGEMENT SKILLS:**

Time management is a skill that many individuals with ADHD find elusive. They may need help estimating the time required for tasks and often underestimate how long they will take to complete them. This can lead to chronic lateness, missed deadlines, and a sense of constantly being rushed.

- **DIFFICULTY FOLLOWING INSTRUCTIONS OR REMEMBERING DETAILS:**

Following instructions and remembering details can be challenging for individuals with ADHD. They may need help to process and retain verbal or written instructions, leading to errors and misunderstandings. This can be particularly problematic in academic and work settings where accuracy and attention to detail are essential.

- **EASILY DISTRACTED BY EXTERNAL STIMULI:**

Individuals with ADHD are highly susceptible to distractions from external stimuli. Even seemingly minor noises, movements, or visual stimuli can divert their attention and disrupt their concentration. This sensitivity to distractions can make it difficult to engage in tasks that require sustained focus, such as reading, studying, or working on complex projects.

- **AGGRESSION, MOODINESS, OR IRRITABILITY:**

Emotional dysregulation is a challenge that some individuals with ADHD face. They may experience mood swings, irritability, and emotional outbursts, especially when frustrated or overwhelmed by their symptoms. This emotional volatility can sometimes lead to aggression or conflict with others.

- **ACADEMIC AND SOCIAL IMPLICATIONS:**

The signs and symptoms of ADHD can profoundly impact various aspects of an individual's life, including academic performance and social relationships. Many individuals with ADHD struggle with homework assignments and studying for tests due to their difficulty with focus and task completion. This can result in lower academic achievement than their peers who do not face the same challenges, even if they have similar cognitive abilities.

In social settings, individuals with ADHD may encounter difficulties due to their limited ability to pay attention during conversations or to stay focused during activities or tasks. These challenges can lead to feelings of frustration, isolation, and strained interpersonal relationships.

It is important to recognize that ADHD is a highly treatable condition. Early diagnosis and appropriate interventions, including behavioral therapy, counseling, medication, and educational support, can significantly improve an individual's ability to manage symptoms and lead a fulfilling life. Understanding the signs and symptoms of ADHD is the first step towards providing the necessary support and resources to those affected by this condition.

DIAGNOSIS OF ADHD

ADHD is typically diagnosed in childhood, though it can persist into adulthood. A diagnosis of ADHD is made through a combination of the individual's medical history and an assessment of their current symptoms. This process usually involves interviews with parents, teachers, or other people close to the individual, along with psychological tests that measure impulsive behavior and attention span.

It is important to note that there are no specific tests used to diagnose ADHD – rather, it is a diagnosis based on observation and evaluation. Therefore, it is crucial to obtain an accurate diagnosis from a qualified health professional in order to get proper treatment and support.

In order for a child to be diagnosed with ADHD, they must have at least 6 symptoms of either inattentiveness or hyperactivity/impulsiveness; these symptoms must have been present for at least 6 months, started before the age of 12, and been observed in at least two different settings. Finally, these symptoms must also be causing significant difficulty in social, academic, or occupational life – not just part of a developmental disorder or hard phase.

TREATMENT OPTIONS

Once an accurate diagnosis has been made, there are a variety of treatment options available for ADHD. This can range from lifestyle changes such as regular exercise and establishing better study habits to medication depending on the severity of the individual's symptoms.

Behavioral therapy is a form of psychotherapy that focuses on teaching individuals how to alter their behaviors and responses to certain stimuli in order to improve focus and attention span and help manage impulsivity. This type of therapy can also be beneficial for managing aggression or mood swings associated with ADHD. It is important to note that behavioral therapy does not provide an immediate solution but requires consistent effort over time before any results are seen.

In some cases, medication may be prescribed alongside behavioral therapy in order to supplement treatment options for ADHD-related symptoms. Medications used to treat ADHD can help increase focus and attention as well as reduce impulsive behaviors. These medications can be stimulants or non-stimulants and are typically taken orally. Commonly prescribed stimulants include methylphenidate and amphetamine.

It is important to speak with a qualified health professional before starting any medication regimen, as the risks and side effects must be weighed against the potential benefits. Common side effects of medications used to treat ADHD include sleep difficulties, loss of appetite or weight gain, increased irritability, headaches, and stomachaches.

In addition to behavioral therapy and/or medication, making lifestyle changes can help manage symptoms associated with ADHD. These include establishing regular routines and study habits, eating healthy meals and snacks on a regular basis, getting enough sleep each night, setting realistic goals that are achievable in manageable increments, avoiding distractions while studying or working on tasks, breaking down large projects into smaller tasks, and engaging in physical activity at least once a day.

REAL-LIFE STORIES OF PEOPLE WITH ADHD

They say it takes a special kind of person to be the best. An individual with an unrivaled drive, ambition, and dedication to their craft. But who could have ever guessed that this person also happened to suffer from a condition like ADHD?

This individual was diagnosed at age nine, yet still managed to rise up against the odds to become one of the greatest athletes ever known. Despite difficulties in concentrating and focusing, he was able to channel his energy into something productive, finding relief in a certain activity: swimming.

Such rigorous training and practice paid off as this individual set a record for most Olympic medals won (28) - 23 of which were gold - and has yet to be surpassed.

He is an inspiration, defying the odds and showing us what is possible with hard work, determination, and perseverance. And his name? Michael Phelps. His story is proof that anything can be achieved when you put your mind to it. He stands out amongst sports legends today and will continue to do so tomorrow.

Adam Levine, the celebrated frontman of Maroon 5 and host of the hit show "The Voice", is no stranger to struggles with Attention Deficit Hyperactivity Disorder (ADHD). In an article he wrote for Additude magazine, Levine discussed his difficulties with attention as a child and how it has followed him into adulthood.

From an early age, Levine experienced challenges that his peers did not have to face — such as sitting still and completing work in school or focusing on tasks at home. His parents worked hard to help their son find treatment options that would best fit his needs; however, these issues persisted through his teenage years and even into adulthood.

It is clear that although ADHD is largely viewed as a condition that affects children and young adults, it can follow people throughout their lives if left untreated. With Levine's public platform, he is helping to raise awareness about this condition by sharing his story with others whose lives have been impacted by ADHD.

Levine's story offers hope for those who are struggling with the disorder or know someone who is dealing with it. He explains that although there have been many difficult days in managing his own condition, he has learned effective coping strategies over time which have helped him manage his symptoms better. This includes making sure he gets enough to sleep each night and creating a schedule for himself to stay organized and productive throughout the day.

Today, Adam Levine remains committed to making sure people living with ADHD feel heard and understood. He believes in the power of speaking up about mental health issues and uses his personal experiences to bring greater awareness on the subject hoping to provide support for those who may need it most.

Simone Bile's gold medal performance in the 2016 Olympics was a major win for people with Attention Deficit Hyperactivity Disorder (ADHD). After it was revealed that Biles had tested positive for methylphenidate (Ritalin), a medication used to treat ADHD, the world celebrated her achievement and praised her courage in speaking up about her diagnosis.

Biles' story is inspiring because she has been living with ADHD since she was a child and did not let it limit her success. Her parents found resources to help their daughter cope with the disorder, such as using stimulant medications, practicing task-switching when working on tasks, breaking down large projects into smaller tasks, and engaging in physical activity at least once a day.

CHAPTER 4
OBSESSIVE COMPULSIVE DISORDER

Obsessive-Compulsive Disorder (OCD) is a complex and distressing anxiety disorder that can cast a shadow of relentless worry, fear, and unease over an individual's life. Those afflicted with OCD are burdened by the constant presence of intrusive, unwelcome thoughts that invade their minds like uninvited guests. These intrusive thoughts trigger a compelling urge to engage in repetitive, ritualistic behaviours, whether physical actions like excessive hand-washing or mental rituals like counting or reciting certain phrases.

What sets OCD apart from many other mental health conditions is its uncanny ability to permeate every facet of a person's existence. This disorder does not discriminate; it can manifest in individuals from all walks of life, regardless of age, gender, or cultural background. The relentless cycle of obsessive thoughts and compulsive actions can feel like an inescapable labyrinth, a maze of the mind where the exit remains elusive.

The relentless grip of OCD can render even the most mundane tasks, such as getting dressed or leaving the house, into arduous and time-consuming endeavours. The constant need to engage in these rituals can consume hours each day, leaving little room for pursuing one's goals, hobbies, or social interactions. OCD can turn the simplest of activities into monumental challenges, draining a person's mental and physical energy.

Moreover, the emotional toll is substantial. Those grappling with OCD often experience immense distress, guilt, and shame as they recognize the irrationality of their compulsions but remain powerless to resist them. The fear of dire consequences or harm befalling themselves or their loved ones if they do not perform these rituals can be paralyzing.

In sum, OCD is not just a matter of quirky habits or excessive neatness; it is a formidable adversary that invades the mind and disrupts the rhythm of everyday life. It is a relentless battle between reason and compulsion, where the individual desperately seeks relief from the tormenting thoughts and the relentless urge to perform rituals. Compassion, understanding, and appropriate treatment are essential in helping individuals with OCD regain control of their lives and find the path towards recovery.

CAUSES OF OCD

While the exact cause of OCD remains elusive, research has uncovered a multifaceted interplay of biological and psychological factors, shedding light on the origins of this disorder.

One significant aspect of understanding the causes of OCD lies in genetics. Family studies have provided substantial evidence that OCD can run in families, suggesting a hereditary component. Individuals with a first-degree relative, such as a parent or sibling, who has OCD are at a higher risk of developing the disorder. This familial aggregation suggests that certain genetic factors may predispose individuals to OCD.

Although specific genes have not been definitively identified, research into the genetic basis of OCD continues to advance. Identifying these genes may provide a clearer understanding of the biological underpinnings of the disorder.

Further contributing to the biological perspective is observing structural and functional changes in the brains of individuals with OCD. Neuroimaging studies have revealed abnormalities in various brain regions, particularly the orbitofrontal cortex, anterior cingulate cortex, and basal ganglia. These areas involve decision-making, impulse control, and emotional regulation, which are implicated in OCD symptoms. The basal ganglia, in particular, plays a crucial role in fine-tuning motor movements and habit formation. Dysfunction in this region may explain the repetitive compulsions characteristic of OCD, as individuals may feel compelled to engage in ritualistic behaviours to alleviate anxiety. Moreover, the abnormal connectivity between these brain regions suggests a neural circuitry dysfunction contributing to the developing and maintaining OCD symptoms.

While genetics and brain abnormalities offer critical insights, psychological factors also play a pivotal role in the onset of OCD. Traumatic events, such as abuse or neglect, and highly stressful life experiences have been implicated as environmental factors that can trigger OCD in susceptible individuals. These events may disrupt an individual's emotional and psychological equilibrium, leading to the emergence of obsessive-compulsive symptoms as a coping mechanism. For instance, someone who experiences a traumatic incident may develop obsessions related to contamination and engage in compulsive cleaning rituals to regain control and safety.

Moreover, personality traits can contribute to the development of OCD symptoms. Two prominent traits associated with OCD are perfectionism and difficulty managing emotions. Perfectionists have a strong need for order and control, which can manifest as obsessions related to symmetry or cleanliness. Their compulsive behaviours may be driven by an overwhelming desire to achieve a perceived perfect state. Difficulty managing emotions, on the other hand, can lead to obsessive thoughts that are distressing and hard to dismiss. Compulsions may then be employed to mitigate the distress caused by these obsessions. These personality traits, while not causing OCD alone, can make individuals more susceptible to developing the disorder when combined with other risk factors.

It's essential to recognize that the causes of OCD are not isolated to these individual factors but rather emerge from a complex interplay of genetic, neurological, and psychological elements. Furthermore, the specific combination and weight of these factors can vary from one individual to another, making the aetiology of OCD a highly individualized phenomenon. This multifactorial nature also underscores why OCD can present differently in each person, with a wide range of obsessions and compulsions that may appear unrelated on the surface.

Additionally, recent research has begun to explore the role of the immune system and infections in developing OCD. Some studies have found a potential link between streptococcal infections and the onset of a subtype of OCD known as Pediatric Autoimmune Neuropsychiatric Disorders Associated with Streptococcal Infections (PANDAS). This condition involves sudden and severe OCD symptoms in children following a strep infection. While the exact mechanisms remain under investigation, it suggests that immune responses may play a role in triggering OCD in certain cases.

OCD is a complex and multifaceted disorder with various potential causes. While much progress has been made in understanding its origins, the exact cause remains elusive. Genetic predisposition, neurobiological abnormalities, environmental triggers, personality traits, and potential immune system involvement collectively contribute to the development of OCD. Recognizing the intricate interplay between these factors is essential for a comprehensive understanding of the disorder and for tailoring effective treatments that address the unique needs of individuals living with OCD. Continued research into the causes of OCD is crucial for advancing our understanding of this debilitating condition and developing more targeted and effective interventions for those who suffer from it.

SYMPTOMS

Fear of Contamination or Dirt: One of the most well-known obsessions in OCD is the fear of contamination. The fear of germs, dirt, or contamination from everyday objects, surfaces, or other people may consume individuals with this obsession. This fear can lead to compulsive behaviours such as excessive hand washing or avoidance of certain situations or places.

Doubts About Completing Tasks Correctly: Another common obsession is the fear of making a mistake or not completing a task correctly. People with OCD may doubt whether they turned off the stove, locked the door, or performed other routine actions correctly. This leads to repetitive checking behaviours to ensure everything is in order.

Need for Symmetry or Order: Some individuals with OCD have a compulsion for symmetry and order. They may feel compelled to arrange objects in a specific way or symmetrically perform tasks. Deviating from this perceived order can cause immense distress.

Aggressive or Horrific Thoughts: Intrusive thoughts about harming oneself or others are distressing and common obsessions in OCD. Despite having no intention of acting on these thoughts, individuals with OCD may be plagued by images or fears of losing control and causing harm to themselves or loved ones.

Unwanted Sexual Images: Another OCD obsession involves unwanted sexual thoughts or images disturbing and distressing the individual. These thoughts can be deeply distressing and lead to compulsions to neutralise them.

Fear of Shouting Obscenities or Acting Inappropriately: Some individuals with OCD experience obsessions about shouting obscenities or behaving inappropriately in public. These thoughts can cause significant anxiety and shame, leading to compulsive efforts to suppress or neutralize them.

Avoidance and Safety Behaviors: To prevent triggering their obsessions, individuals with OCD may engage in avoidance behaviours. For example, someone who fears contamination may avoid touching objects touched by others or avoid crowded places. These avoidance behaviours can significantly limit one's daily life and social interactions.

THE CYCLE OF OBSESSIONS AND COMPULSIONS

The hallmark of OCD is the cycle of obsessions and compulsions. Obsessions cause intense anxiety and discomfort, leading individuals to engage in compulsive behaviours to temporarily alleviate this distress. However, these compulsions provide only short-term relief and reinforce the belief that performing them is necessary to prevent harm or catastrophe. This cycle perpetuates the disorder and can be immensely disruptive to daily life.

THE BATTLE WITHIN COPING WITH OCD

Living with OCD can be described as a constant battle within one's mind. Individuals with OCD often recognize that their obsessions and compulsions are irrational and excessive, yet they feel powerless to control them. The anxiety and distress associated with OCD can be overwhelming, leading to a significant decrease in the quality of life.

In extreme cases, OCD can interfere with daily functioning, work, relationships, and overall wellbeing. Rituals and compulsions can take up much time, leaving little room for other activities and interests. People with OCD may also face stigma and misunderstanding from others who do not fully grasp their internal torment.

DIAGNOSIS AND TREATMENT

Obsessive Compulsive Disorder is diagnosed by a mental health professional who evaluates the patient's symptoms and makes an assessment based on their observations. A diagnosis of OCD can be made if the person's obsessions and compulsions are causing significant distress, interfering with daily activities and social relationships, or when they take up more than one hour per day.

The primary treatment for OCD involves a combination of medications, such as selective serotonin reuptake inhibitors (SSRIs), and psychotherapy, such as Cognitive Behavioral Therapy (CBT) and Exposure and Response Prevention (ERP).

Medications are used to reduce anxiety and decrease the frequency of obsessive thoughts and compulsive behavior. SSRIs are the most common type of medication prescribed for OCD, as they work by affecting the neurotransmitters that regulate moods. Other medications used in treating OCD include tricyclic antidepressants, atypical antipsychotics, and benzodiazepines.

CBT is an evidence-based form of psychotherapy that focuses on changing unhelpful thinking patterns associated with OCD. It often combines exposure techniques with cognitive restructuring techniques to help reduce anxiety stemming from obsessions or compulsions.

ERP therapy, also known as Exposure and Response Prevention, is a type of behavioral therapy used to treat patients with Obsessive Compulsive Disorder (OCD). In this approach, the patient is gradually exposed to situations that evoke the urge to perform their rituals while simultaneously resisting the urge to complete them. This technique allows a person with OCD to gain control over their fear and anxiety, thereby reducing their compulsion to carry out behaviors that they have come to associate with safety.

In ERP therapy, the patient is first provided with educational information about OCD and its treatment. Therapists then help the patient identify situations that elicit compulsions, such as being in crowded areas or coming in contact with certain objects or substances. Through gradual exposure, the patient learns how to stay in these situations without having the urge or feeling compelled to act out their rituals.

ERP therapy can be conducted either individually or in a group setting. When done in a group setting, members are taught how to challenge each other's irrational thoughts and develop more adaptive coping strategies. This helps create an atmosphere of mutual support and understanding where individuals feel comfortable discussing their experiences of fear and anxiety associated with OCD symptoms.

Cognitive restructuring techniques are also used during ERP sessions. These strategies help patients learn how to recognize patterns in their thoughts that lead them towards performing compulsions, so they can then find healthier ways of responding that do not involve performing rituals. For instance, if someone has an obsession with dirtiness and washes his hands every time he touches something dirty, his therapist might suggest replacing this behavior by using hand sanitizer instead.

Finally, relaxation techniques are incorporated into ERP sessions as well since intense emotional states like fear and anxiety can increase the intensity of compulsive behavior. Progressive muscle relaxation is one example of an effective exercise for reducing tension throughout the body which may help lessen distress caused by obsessions or compulsions.

Complementary therapies such as relaxation techniques and yoga can also be helpful in managing symptoms of OCD. Additionally, self-help strategies such as organizing one's environment and setting aside specific times during the day to focus on obsessions can help manage symptoms effectively.

Overall, it is important for individuals with OCD to learn how to recognize their triggers, challenge negative thought patterns, resist compulsions, build resilience toward distressing stimuli, and embrace healthy coping strategies in order to effectively manage their disorder. With a proper diagnosis from a mental health professional combined with appropriate treatment plans tailored to each individual's needs, individuals may be able to live without significant disruption from their symptoms over the long term.

AN ACCOUNT OF A FEW PEOPLE WHO HAD SYMPTOMS OF OCD

Donald Trump is a living example of someone struggling with Obsessive Compulsive Disorder (OCD). While his political career led to handshaking becoming an integral part of his public life, it was something he initially struggled with. The fear of germs and the idea that teachers were particularly infected was enough to make him avoid any kind of physical contact.

Fortunately, Donald Trump has found ways to live with this disorder while still maintaining his reputation as a clean and tidy individual. As such, it serves as an inspiration for anyone else dealing with OCD to know that they can find ways to get around their obstacles, no matter how daunting they may seem.

It began with ungrateful thoughts and a deep-seated shame that didn't feel right. As these intrusive thoughts grew more intense, an artist and songwriter knew she needed help. Through cognitive behavioral therapy, meditation, and self-care strategies, this person found the strength to better understand her own experience with Obsessive Compulsive Disorder.

With hard work and dedication, this individual gained insight into how to manage her OCD in daily life. Encouraging others to talk openly about their struggles with mental health, just like one would do for physical health issues, was important for breaking down the stigma and shame surrounding it. Now, this artist uses her own experience to bring awareness to the disorder and advocates for a greater understanding of mental health issues.

That artist is Camila Cabello. With her honesty and courage, she has helped others gain peace in their own lives while facing OCD.

The story of an iconic figure, renowned for his comedic wit, hosting prowess, and acting talent. Despite his success in the public eye, he suffered from a debilitating mental illness - one that manifested itself through irrational fears of dirt or contamination. He was so overwhelmed by intrusive thoughts that he would do mundane things like checking if the door was locked thirty times in one session.

This person never spoke publicly of his struggles until he made a conscious effort to destigmatize mental illnesses and encourage dialogue about such issues - something that has become a major part of his mission ever since.

The figure we've been talking about is none other than Howie Mandel - a man who continues to break the stigma surrounding mental health and inspire open conversation about these issues.

David Beckham, a legendary soccer star, is known for his impressive career and iconic style.

However, what many people may not know is that he has lived with Obsessive Compulsive Disorder (OCD) since childhood. This disorder has shaped the way he lives and affects his daily life in ways that most people don't experience.

Beckham compulsively arranges things in a particular order or pattern – from color-coded clothes to specific orientations of furniture. He also gets overwhelmed by intrusive thoughts and irrational fears. For example, once he threw away a can of soda because he wanted to have an even number of two items on the table. On another occasion, he bought three refrigerators to avoid having other things mixed in with the food he was storing.

Despite his best efforts, Beckham has been unable to stop these patterns of behavior. This condition can be debilitating and cause a great deal of stress and disruption in daily life. He has had to accept that this part of his identity is something he will have to live with for the rest of his life.

Many of the world's most famous people, despite their success and the sparkle around their lives, have walked through the darkness of mental health challenges. These are folks who appear to have it all, yet behind the surface, they battle inner demons that many of us can identify with. Their willingness to share their tales brings the problem of mental health into the spotlight, reminding the audience that even behind the smiles, honors, and triumphs, the mind can be a place of agony.

One of the most extensively discussed stories is that of Robin Williams. A renowned actor and comedian who provided humor and joy to millions, Robin was privately dealing with serious depression and mental health challenges. His apparent joy and ability to make others smile disguised an interior maelstrom. Robin was known for his improvisational brilliance and iconic parts in films like *Good Will Hunting* and *Dead Poets Society*. However, his genius on screen was balanced by tremendous grief in his private life. As he publicly spoke about his issues with addiction and despair, he touched on a struggle many didn't expect from someone so full of life and enthusiasm. His untimely passing in 2014 was a stark reminder of how profound and severe mental illness can be, even for someone who seemed larger than life.

Similar to Robin, another prominent musician, Lady Gaga, has openly shared her difficulties with mental health. The pop artist, famed for her colorful dress and amazing singing talent, claimed that she struggled with PTSD and despair. Her honesty in talking about these concerns made her a champion for mental health, especially as she ascended to popularity. Gaga explained how her trauma, originating from a sexual attack early in her career, had long-lasting ramifications on her mental well-being. Despite her accomplishments, she faced days where getting out of bed felt difficult. But her tale is one of perseverance, as she uses her platform not simply to entertain but to fight for mental health awareness and inspire others to get assistance without shame.

Then there's Dwayne "The Rock" Johnson, a man whose persona radiates strength and positivity. He has been upfront about his battle with depression despite the exterior image of being a powerhouse, both physically and emotionally. Known for his professional wrestling career and successful move into Hollywood, Johnson said that after his football career ended prematurely, he plunged into a profound despair, feeling that his aspirations were ruined. He spoke openly about how, even with his current success, he has had periods where he felt alienated and hopeless. His transparency has influenced many to see that it's normal not always to be OK, no matter how strong you appear on the outside.

Selena Gomez is another singer who has become a light for mental health activism. At an early age, Selena was thrown into the spotlight as a Disney star, and her transition to adulthood was marked by great strain. She has fought with anxiety, sadness, and lupus, an autoimmune condition that not only impacts her physically but also takes a toll on her mental health. Gomez made the daring decision to take vacations from her work to prioritize her well-being, seeking therapy and spending time in treatment centers. Her story serves as a strong reminder that no one is immune to mental illness, and getting treatment is a show of strength, not weakness.

Another musician who shattered the silence around mental health is Kanye West. The rapper and producer has been a figure of both admiration and controversy, and his problems with bipolar disease have been a crucial aspect of his public existence. In recent years, Kanye has spoken about his experiences with manic episodes, which have often played out in the public glare, leaving fans and the media divided in their impressions of his behavior. Through his music and interviews, Kanye has attempted to de-stigmatize mental illness, showing that managing bipolar disorder is a lifetime struggle. His capacity to continue creating art, despite the unpredictability of his health, speaks to his perseverance, even if his journey has been laden with hardships.

One of the most poignant stories comes from the domain of monarchy. Prince Harry, the Duke of Sussex, has been incredibly candid about his difficulties with mental health, particularly in the wake of his mother Princess Diana's terrible death. Losing their mom at such an early age left Harry battling with grief, rage, and confusion. For years, he buried his emotions, only to have them resurface later in life. His choice to speak out about getting therapy and the significance of mental well-being was groundbreaking, especially within the usually stoic ethos of the British royal family. Through his frank interviews and the establishment of projects like Heads Together, Harry has been a forerunner in reframing the discussion about mental health, encouraging others to seek treatment without feeling judged.

Behind the realm of tennis, Naomi Osaka's narrative also sheds a focus on mental health. The young tennis sensation earned headlines not just for her extraordinary ability on the court but for her courage in pulling back from major competitions to focus on her mental well-being. Citing long-standing battles with anxiety and depression, Naomi has been a leading voice in reminding the world that mental health should always come first, especially for athletes who are at the pinnacle of their game. By putting her mental health over the expectations of the world, Osaka set a new precedent in sports, demonstrating that taking care of one's head is as vital as physical training.

In the music industry, Mariah Carey disclosed that she was diagnosed with bipolar disorder. For years, she kept her diagnosis quiet, dreading the stigma that may come with it. However, after years of internal conflicts, she elected to go public, detailing how the disorder affected her mood swings and energy levels. Her narrative is one of self-acceptance and learning to manage a lifelong disease while yet having a successful profession. Mariah's bravery in disclosing such a personal battle gives strength to many who might feel alone in their diagnoses.

Similarly, the British artist Adele has described her experience with postpartum depression after the birth of her son. Though Adele is recognized for her loud voice and presence, she opened up about the isolation and worry that followed her into parenthood. Her honesty in interviews helped mainstream postpartum depression, a condition frequently veiled in obscurity. Adele's tale highlights that even with celebrity and success, the struggles of mental health can impact anyone, and obtaining support is vital.

In the realm of acting, Catherine Zeta-Jones has spoken openly about her diagnosis of bipolar II disorder. The Welsh actress confessed that the dramatic highs and lows of her disease made it impossible to maintain balance in her life. After obtaining therapy, she became an advocate for mental health awareness, utilizing her position to remove stigma and urge others to seek help. Her transparency showed that mental illness is not something to be ashamed of but rather a part of her journey that needs attention and care.

Among younger celebs, Justin Bieber has also been forthright about his mental health. The music phenomenon, who grew up in the limelight, underwent enormous strain and criticism from an early age. As his celebrity grew, so did his anxiety, melancholy, and feelings of inadequacy. Justin's problems culminated in a period of intense contemplation and therapy, during which he learned to manage his mental health through spiritual and professional support. His honesty about his experience, particularly with his fans, helped teach the younger generation that fame does not shelter one from mental health difficulties.

Beyond the world of acting and music, sports figures have also shared their mental health battles. One such individual is Michael Phelps, the most decorated Olympian of all time. With 28 Olympic medals, Phelps seemed invincible in the pool, but behind his success was a man struggling deeply with depression. After the 2012 Olympics, Phelps admitted that he had reached his lowest point and even contemplated suicide. The pressure to perform and the intense isolation that followed the end of each competition cycle made him feel lost. His decision to speak openly about his experiences with depression, anxiety, and ADHD transformed him from a champion swimmer to a champion of mental health awareness. By sharing his story, Phelps helped break down the misconception that athletes are immune to mental health struggles, reminding the world that mental well-being is just as important as physical fitness.

Similarly, Kevin Love, an NBA star, made headlines when he opened up about his panic attacks during a game. The Cleveland Cavaliers player, known for his resilience on the basketball court, shocked many when he wrote about his struggles with anxiety and depression in a deeply personal essay. Love explained how mental illness doesn't discriminate, even among the strongest athletes. His vulnerability opened doors for more athletes to discuss their mental health issues, creating a culture of acceptance in sports where such conversations were once considered taboo. His courage to speak up reminded fans and fellow athletes alike that it's OK not to be OK and that seeking help is a sign of strength, not weakness.

In the fashion world, model Cara Delevingne has been vocal about her struggles with depression and self-harm. From the outside, Cara's life seemed like a dream — she was one of the world's most successful models, walking runways for top designers and gracing magazine covers. But behind her success was a young woman grappling with feelings of worthlessness and deep sadness. Delevingne explained that she struggled with depression from a young age, feeling overwhelmed by the pressures of the industry and societal expectations. She sought therapy and eventually stepped back from the spotlight to prioritize her mental health. Her story resonated with many young people who also felt the weight of expectations and reminded them that it's OK to slow down and take care of their mental well-being.

In the tech world, Elon Musk, the entrepreneur behind Tesla and SpaceX, has also touched on his experiences with mental health. Known for his ambitious projects and innovative mind, Musk has hinted at his struggles with depression and burnout. While he rarely delves deep into the subject, Musk's acknowledgment of the mental toll that comes with high-stakes leadership offers a glimpse into the vulnerabilities that even the most successful individuals face. His experience shows that, even in industries like technology and business, mental health is a crucial part of sustaining long-term success.

Both Emma Stone and Billie Eilish have become influential figures in the discourse surrounding mental health. They have revealed their own experiences with anxiety and sadness in a way that has motivated countless others. For many of their followers, their honesty has de-stigmatized mental health concerns and raised awareness of them. They demonstrate that it is possible to manage mental health issues while still achieving personal and professional goals by being open and honest about their experiences.

Emma Stone has struggled with anxiety her whole life, even when she was a little child. Emma started having severe panic episodes when she was seven years old, which made her feel scared and helpless. She would frequently experience these attacks without notice, which made her think uncontrollably wild and detached from reality. She has characterized the experience of panic as horrifying in interviews, describing her body feeling like it was betraying her, her mind rushing, and her heart pounding. Irrational anxieties would overtake her, leading her to believe that something terrible was going to happen.

Emma experienced anxiety on a regular basis rather than merely being a passing sensation of uneasiness. She described how her panic episodes would occasionally keep her from engaging in typical childhood activities, which made her feel alone and different from other children. Her head filled with anxiety and concern, making her world appear smaller.

Emma's parents assisted her in seeking therapy at an early age after realizing the intensity of her anxiety. She started to develop strategies and tools in treatment that would enable her to regain control in panicked situations. Deep breathing exercises were one of the best tactics for her as they helped to relax her nervous system and bring her back to the present. She also picked up grounding exercises, including paying attention to her breath or concentrating on tactile experiences like touching a surface. She was able to stabilize herself thanks to these routines while she was experiencing extreme anxiety.

Emma kept working to control her anxiousness while her Hollywood career took off. She has talked about how acting gave her a platform to express her feelings and gave her a sense of direction. She felt in control of the strength of her sentiments since acting provided her with a controlled atmosphere in which to explore her emotions. Emma learned to accept her fear and channel it into inspiration for her artistic endeavors, even if it never completely went away.

Emma has utilized her platform to talk candidly about her issues with anxiety throughout her journey. By sharing her experience, she hopes to inspire others who are dealing with comparable problems to get support and realize they are not alone. Many of her followers, especially those who have felt alone due to their mental health issues, have found solace in her honesty. Emma's transparency has had a significant influence in a society where stigmatization and misunderstanding of mental health concerns are common.

Even though Billie Eilish's narrative differs from Emma's, it nonetheless highlights the need for mental health advocacy. Billie, being a worldwide pop phenomenon, has been under constant scrutiny and strain since her early years. When she first became well-known as a teenager, the spotlight was focused entirely on her. Few people were aware of Billie's troubles behind the scenes, despite the fact that many recognized her as a gifted and edgy young artist.

Billie has been open about her struggles with body dysmorphia and depression, which were made worse by her unexpected ascent to stardom. She has discussed how her mental health issues became more severe as a result of her celebrity, frequently causing her to feel estranged from her body and self. She occasionally had the impression that, despite her achievements, she was always struggling with thoughts of inadequacy and self-doubt. Billie experienced severe depressive episodes as a result of the enormous pressure to uphold a particular image on both a physical and creative level.

As a public child, Billie was subjected to continuous criticism about her beauty. Body dysmorphia, a disorder in which a person becomes obsessed with perceived imperfections in their appearance, was brought on by the inspection of her body. This was an extremely terrible event for Billie, and it made her feel disassociated from her own body. She has talked about how challenging it was to deal with these emotions and pursue her profession and musical endeavors at the same time.

Despite the difficulties, Billie attributes her family's support—especially her brother Finneas—to assisting her in overcoming her mental health issues. She has also found comfort in counseling, where she acquired skills to control her body dysmorphia and despair. For Billie, music has also been a lifeline, giving her a way to communicate with people who might be going through similar things and express her thoughts.

Particularly for her younger admirers, Billie's choice to be transparent about her mental health has had a significant effect. She has demonstrated that even those who appear to have everything may still suffer from serious inner conflicts by opening up about her challenges. Her supporters have been able to feel seen and understood by her vulnerability, which serves as a reminder that it's acceptable not to feel okay. The stigma associated with depression and body image problems has also been lessened because of Billie's openness about her mental health, which has promoted more candid discussions about these subjects.

Emma Stone and Billie Eilish have demonstrated that mental health issues are universal and may impact individuals of all backgrounds and social statuses. Through sharing their narratives, they have not only increased awareness but also given hope to those facing comparable difficulties. Their openness has made it simpler for others to seek support and assistance by normalizing talks about mental health.

In a society where mental health concerns are frequently ignored, Emma and Billie's courageous decision to speak up has had a huge impact. They have demonstrated that it is feasible to pursue one's goals in life while having anxiety, sadness, and body dysmorphia. Their experiences serve as potent reminders that getting assistance is a show of strength rather than weakness and that mental health is equally as vital as physical health.

The expectation is that the stigma associated with mental health disorders will continue to decline as more and more well-known people come forward to discuss their experiences with it. Leading the charge in this movement are Billie Eilish and Emma Stone, who use their platforms to promote mental health care and awareness. Numerous people have been motivated to take charge of their mental health by their tales, which demonstrate that anybody can overcome any obstacle with the correct resources and assistance.

J.K. Rowling, the author behind the Harry Potter series, also battled depression during her rise to fame. Before publishing her first book, Rowling was a single mother living in poverty, struggling with the weight of depression. She has spoken openly about how she felt like she was "drowning" during that period of her life, describing her mental illness as a "presence" that would sap her energy and motivation. Writing became her escape, and the success of the Harry Potter series gave her a new sense of purpose. But even with her newfound success, Rowling continued to prioritize her mental health, speaking openly about her depression and encouraging others to seek help when they need it.

Similarly, Ryan Reynolds, the actor known for his roles in Deadpool and The Proposal, has discussed his experiences with anxiety. Despite his humorous and lighthearted persona, Reynolds has dealt with intense bouts of anxiety throughout his career. He often feels pressure to perform, which has led to sleepless nights and feelings of overwhelming stress. Reynolds credits therapy and a strong support system for helping him manage his anxiety, reminding his fans that mental health struggles can exist even in the midst of success and fame.

In the world of comedy, Jim Carrey, one of the most recognizable comedians in Hollywood, has shared his battle with depression. Known for his slapstick humor and over-the-top characters, Carrey's life off-screen was far more complex. He described how, despite his success, he often felt a deep sense of emptiness. At times, his depression became so debilitating that he needed to take medication to cope. Carrey's story shows that even those who bring laughter to the world can experience deep emotional pain, and his journey toward mental wellness continues to inspire fans around the globe.

Model and actress Chrissy Teigen has also been open about her struggles with postpartum depression. After the birth of her daughter, Luna, Teigen began to feel overwhelmed, isolated, and sad, despite the joy she felt as a new mother. She sought help and began speaking publicly about postpartum depression, helping to de-stigmatize the condition and encouraging other mothers to seek the support they need. Her candidness about her mental health, combined with her relatable personality, has made her a beacon of honesty and openness in the celebrity world.

In the world of television, Ellen DeGeneres, the beloved talk show host, has opened up about the severe depression she faced after publicly coming out as gay in the 1990s. At the height of her career, Ellen took a huge personal and professional risk by revealing her true self to the world, and the backlash was swift. She lost her show, and many doors closed to her. The experience plunged her into depression, and she wondered if she would ever work in Hollywood again. However, Ellen's resilience saw her bounce back, becoming one of the most successful talk show hosts of all time. Her story is one of perseverance and self-acceptance, illustrating that even when the world seems to turn against you, it's possible to come out stronger on the other side.

Pop icon Britney Spears is another celebrity whose mental health struggles have been highly publicized. The pressures of fame from a young age, combined with personal challenges, led to a highly publicized breakdown in 2007. Spears has spoken about her battles with anxiety, depression, and being placed under a conservatorship that lasted over a decade. In recent years, Britney has regained control of her life and her narrative, sharing her journey with the world and reclaiming her autonomy. Her story is a complex one, marked by both struggle and resilience and serves as a reminder of the toll that fame can take on mental health.

Hollywood star Leonardo DiCaprio has also touched on his experiences with obsessive-compulsive disorder (OCD). Known for his meticulous approach to acting, DiCaprio has spoken about how his obsessive tendencies have impacted his life, making him feel compelled to perform certain rituals and routines. Despite the challenges, DiCaprio has managed to channel his perfectionism into his craft, becoming one of the most respected actors of his generation. His willingness to talk about OCD has helped shine a light on the disorder, helping others who struggle with similar compulsions feel less alone.

British singer Zayn Malik, formerly of One Direction, has opened up about his battle with anxiety. After leaving the band, Malik revealed that the pressure of fame, coupled with intense touring schedules, exacerbated his anxiety, sometimes preventing him from performing. Malik's openness about his mental health has been praised by fans and the media alike, showing that it's OK to prioritize mental well-being, even when it means stepping back from the limelight. His story has resonated particularly with young men, who often feel societal pressure to remain silent about their mental health struggles.

The late singer Amy Winehouse's struggles with addiction and mental health were tragically well-documented. Known for her soulful voice and hits like "Rehab," Winehouse battled substance abuse, depression, and bulimia throughout much of her career. Despite her immense talent, her demons eventually took a toll, and she passed away in 2011 at the age of 27. Winehouse's story serves as a cautionary tale about the dangers of untreated mental illness and addiction, as well as the importance of support systems and early intervention.

Finally, renowned chef and television personality Anthony Bourdain was another public figure whose mental health struggles ended in tragedy. Bourdain, who brought the world's diverse cultures and cuisines into living rooms across the globe, was known for his wit, intellect, and insatiable curiosity. However, behind the scenes, he battled depression for much of his life. His unexpected passing in 2018 was a stark reminder that mental illness can affect anyone, even those who seem to have it all.

In conclusion, Obsessive Compulsive Disorder is a complex mental health condition that can have serious impacts on a person's life. It is important to seek help if you feel like you are struggling with OCD, as cognitive-behavioral therapy and medications are effective treatments for this disorder. Many people find success in managing their symptoms by using the tools they learn through treatment along with lifestyle changes such as creating a structured daily routine and prioritizing self-care. Though it may be difficult, remember that recovery from OCD is possible. With the right support system and resources available to them, individuals living with OCD can find freedom from their obsessions and compulsions.

CHAPTER 5
POST TRAUMATIC STRESS DISORDER (PTSD)

Post-Traumatic Stress Disorder (PTSD) is a complex and debilitating mental health condition that can take root in the psyche of anyone who has been exposed to or directly witnessed an event that inflicts intense fear, helplessness, or profound horror. The triggers for PTSD are wide-ranging, encompassing a spectrum of traumatic experiences ranging from the aftermath of natural disasters like earthquakes and hurricanes to the horrors of abuse, violence, or warfare. This disorder profoundly impacts the emotional well-being and daily functioning of those affected by it.

The hallmark of PTSD is the indelible imprint of traumatic events on a person's mental landscape. These events, often beyond one's control, can leave deep emotional scars that persist long after the physical danger has passed. Individuals with PTSD find themselves grappling with many psychological and emotional challenges.

One of the central challenges faced by individuals with PTSD is the regulation of their emotions. The emotional turmoil wrought by traumatic memories can be overwhelming, leading to intense and often unpredictable reactions. Feelings of fear, anger, sadness, and anxiety can surge to the forefront of consciousness at seemingly innocuous triggers, making it exceptionally challenging to maintain emotional stability.

Moreover, the emotional distress stemming from PTSD can infiltrate the very fabric of daily life. Mundane tasks and routine activities can become monumental hurdles as individuals grapple with the relentless onslaught of memories, nightmares, and intrusive thoughts. These persistent reminders of the traumatic event can be so vivid and distressing that they transport the individual back to the moment of the trauma, causing a visceral and debilitating sense of reliving the experience.

The pervasive nature of PTSD can also erode an individual's sense of safety and trust in the world. Heightened alertness and hypervigilance may become the norm as individuals constantly scan their environment for potential threats, even when none exist. This hypervigilance can result in chronic fatigue and a profound sense of isolation, as the world outside is perceived as dangerous and unpredictable.

PTSD is a profound psychological and emotional wound that lingers long after the traumatic event has ended. It disrupts the lives of those affected, making navigating even the simplest of daily tasks challenging. Understanding, compassion, and therapeutic interventions are crucial in helping individuals with PTSD embark on healing and reclaiming their emotional well-being.

SYMPTOMS OF PTSD

People who suffer from PTSD can experience a variety of symptoms that may impact their daily lives. These symptoms can manifest in different ways and vary in intensity, but they are generally grouped into four main categories: intrusive memories, avoidance, negative changes in thinking and mood, and changes in emotional reactions.

Intrusive memories refer to flashbacks or nightmares about the traumatic event(s). This can include reliving the traumatic event through vivid images or sensations, having strong emotions related to the event such as fear or anger, as well as feeling detached from oneself when experiencing these intense emotions. People with PTSD may also try to avoid anything that could bring back memories of the trauma; people suffering from this condition tend to isolate themselves from friends and family, or simply avoid talking about their feelings.

In addition to avoiding the memories of the trauma, people with PTSD may also experience negative changes in thinking and mood. These can include difficulty concentrating, feeling guilty or ashamed for surviving the traumatic event(s), feeling emotionally numb, as well as having thoughts of suicide.

Finally, changes in emotional reactions may include being easily startled or angered by even minor events, feeling detached from close relationships, having trouble expressing emotions (particularly joy), and an inability to feel pleasure in activities that used to bring happiness prior to experiencing the trauma.

Although these symptoms are not uncommon after experiencing a traumatic event such as abuse or natural disaster, if they persist for more than four weeks and cause significant distress or disruption to daily life, it is likely that PTSD may be present.

CAUSES AND RISK FACTORS

Post-Traumatic Stress Disorder (PTSD) is a complex and debilitating mental health disorder that can manifest in individuals due to exposure to various traumatic events. These distressing experiences encompass various life-altering situations, such as physical or emotional abuse, natural disasters, combat exposure, or the harrowing act of witnessing a severe accident. The aftermath of such events can profoundly impact an individual's mental well-being, leading to the onset of PTSD.

While it is essential to recognize that anyone can potentially develop PTSD following a traumatic incident, certain factors increase an individual's vulnerability to this disorder. Notably, individuals who have previously grappled with depression or other anxiety disorders are at an elevated risk of developing PTSD when confronted with subsequent traumatic events. The intertwining of preexisting psychological vulnerabilities can create a fertile ground for the emergence of this condition.

Moreover, prolonged periods of intense stress or overwhelming fear before encountering a traumatic incident can heighten the likelihood of developing PTSD. The cumulative burden of emotional strain can erode an individual's resilience, making them more susceptible to the psychological scars left in the wake of trauma.

Furthermore, a particularly poignant and concerning risk factor for PTSD is a history of childhood trauma. Individuals who endured physical or emotional abuse and neglect or were exposed to violence during their formative years are at an increased risk of grappling with this debilitating disorder in adulthood. The echoes of childhood trauma can reverberate throughout an individual's life, leaving them vulnerable to the lingering effects of PTSD.

In essence, PTSD is a condition that arises from the complex interplay of individual vulnerabilities and the traumatic events they experience. Recognizing these risk factors is crucial in facilitating early intervention and support for those at risk and understanding the intricate nature of this challenging mental health disorder.

COMPLICATIONS OF PTSD

Post-Traumatic Stress Disorder (PTSD) is a profoundly impactful condition that, when left untreated, can lead to a cascade of serious and far-reaching complications. These complications encompass physical and mental health challenges, and their consequences can permeate various aspects of an individual's life.

One of the most concerning complications associated with untreated PTSD is the exacerbation of mental health issues. Individuals grappling with PTSD often battle persistent depression and anxiety. The weight of traumatic memories can cast a shadow over their daily lives, leading to overwhelming feelings of despair and hopelessness. Tragically, the emotional turmoil can escalate to the point where thoughts of suicide become a distressing reality for some. The profound psychological distress can create a dangerous mental landscape, underscoring the urgency of seeking intervention and support.

To cope with the overwhelming symptoms of PTSD, individuals may resort to high-risk behaviours, such as substance abuse involving drugs or alcohol. This maladaptive coping mechanism offers temporary relief but perpetuates a vicious cycle of addiction, worsening their overall well-being.

Furthermore, the interpersonal ramifications of PTSD are noteworthy. People suffering from this condition may struggle to form and maintain close relationships. The constant fear and hypervigilance that often accompany PTSD can make it challenging to trust and feel safe around others. Additionally, the emotional numbing characteristic of PTSD can hinder their ability to express their emotions and connect with others on a meaningful level, further isolating them from vital social support systems.

Physical health can also be compromised in individuals with untreated PTSD. Chronic stress, a hallmark of this condition, affects the body over time. This chronic stress response can lead to the development of debilitating chronic pain disorders such as fibromyalgia and irritable bowel syndrome, adding an extra layer of suffering to an individual's life.

Perhaps most alarmingly, untreated PTSD can have dire consequences for overall physical health. The persistent stress and heightened arousal associated with the disorder can increase the risk of severe health issues, including heart disease, stroke, and diabetes. The toll on the body's systems can be profound and long-lasting, underscoring the imperative nature of early intervention and comprehensive treatment.

The untreated course of PTSD can lead to a compounding series of physical and mental health difficulties, disrupting an individual's life in profound ways. Seeking timely and appropriate treatment for PTSD is essential to mitigate these complications, restore well-being, and prevent the enduring impact of this debilitating disorder on an individual's physical and mental health.

DIAGNOSIS AND TREATMENT

Post-Traumatic Stress Disorder (PTSD) is a serious mental health condition that can have longlasting effects if left untreated. Diagnosis typically involves an assessment of symptoms and how they are impacting the individual's life, as well as their history of exposure to traumatic events. In order to accurately diagnose PTSD, it is important for healthcare professionals to look at the person's overall mental health profile; this includes considering any other conditions present, such as depression or anxiety disorders.

Once diagnosed, treatment for PTSD often involves a combination of psychotherapy and medication. Psychotherapy can help individuals work through their traumatic experiences in a safe and supportive environment; by talking about their feelings, they can gain insight into the root causes of their symptoms and learn to manage them more effectively. Cognitive Behavioral Therapy (CBT) is a form of psychotherapy that focuses on changing negative thought patterns and behaviors in order to reduce anxiety and depression associated with PTSD.

Medications are also used to treat PTSD; typically, these will be antidepressants or anti-anxiety medications. Antidepressants can help improve mood by increasing levels of serotonin in the brain, while anti-anxiety medications help reduce fear and anxiety associated with PTSD. It is important to note that no single drug is effective for everyone; different people may experience varying results from different medication regimens.

In addition to medication and psychotherapy, there are also several alternative therapies that may be used to treat PTSD. Eye Movement Desensitization and Reprocessing (EMDR) is a form of psychotherapy that involves helping the individual process traumatic memories by using eye movements or other forms of tactile stimulation. Mindfulness-Based Stress Reduction (MBSR) is another option; this mindfulness-based approach teaches individuals how to recognize, accept, and manage their symptoms in order to reduce their suffering from PTSD.

Regardless of which treatment option is chosen, it is important for those with PTSD to have access to supportive family and friends who can provide understanding and comfort throughout their recovery journey. It can also help them to engage in activities such as yoga, meditation, or even art therapy in order to help them process their feelings and find healthy ways of coping with their symptoms. With the right support, those suffering from PTSD can learn to manage their condition and lead full, productive lives.

AN ACCOUNT OF A FEW PEOPLE WHO HAD PTSD

Whoopi Goldberg is an Emmy and Academy Award-winning actress, comedian, and talk show host who lives with the daily effects of Post Traumatic Stress Disorder (PTSD). Unfortunately, Goldberg's experience with PTSD began at a young age when she witnessed two planes collide in midair. This traumatic event caused her to suffer from severe panic attacks whenever she boards a plane.

In order to cope with her condition, Whoopi Goldberg has publicly shared that she seeks therapy for her PTSD. She credits this form of treatment as helping her "get through" it; by talking about her trauma and its associated emotions in a safe space, she can gain insight into the root causes of her symptoms and learn how to better manage them.

The multi-talented Barbara Streisand has achieved immense success throughout her career as a singer, actress, and celebrity. However, alongside her accolades and achievements is a story of resilience; Streisand suffers from Post Traumatic Stress Disorder (PTSD). Her journey with PTSD began after one particular performance in Central Park where she forgot the lyrics to a song she was singing. This traumatic event caused Streisand to develop an intense fear of performing live for many years afterward.

Fortunately, with the help of therapy and medication for her condition, Streisand was eventually able to overcome this fear and return to the stage after a 30-year absence. Although she still experiences anxiety from time to time when performing, she is grateful for the progress she has made and is now able to view each performance as an opportunity for growth.

Through her example, Streisand proves that recovery from PTSD is possible; and when faced with immense challenges, resilience always finds a way. Other famous people with PTSD include Lady Gaga, Shia LaBeouf, Ariana Grande, and Charlize Theron.

John is a military veteran who served in a combat zone during a conflict. During his deployment, he witnessed intense combat situations and lost close friends in the line of duty. After returning home, he began experiencing vivid and distressing flashbacks of the war, frequent nightmares, and hypervigilance. Simple everyday noises triggered panic attacks, making it challenging for him to reintegrate into civilian life. With support from a veterans' support group and therapy, John eventually found ways to cope with his PTSD symptoms and regain stability.

Emily suffered from childhood trauma due to physical and emotional abuse from her caregivers. Growing up, she struggled with severe anxiety, trust issues, and a deep sense of unworthiness. These traumatic experiences profoundly affected her ability to form healthy relationships. Through years of therapy, she worked on processing her trauma, building self-esteem, and learning healthier coping mechanisms. Emily's journey toward healing was long and challenging, but it ultimately helped her overcome many of the obstacles caused by her early trauma.

Maria lived through a devastating natural disaster when a hurricane destroyed her home. The traumatic event left her feeling helpless and terrified. Following the disaster, she developed symptoms of PTSD, including severe anxiety whenever storm clouds gathered. She also experienced intrusive thoughts about the hurricane and a constant state of alertness. With the help of therapy focused on trauma processing and exposure therapy, Maria gradually regained her sense of safety and control over her life.

David was involved in a serious car accident that resulted in losing a loved one. The traumatic incident left him with both physical injuries and emotional scars. He developed symptoms of PTSD, including flashbacks to the accident, severe anxiety while driving, and avoidance of certain roads. David sought therapy to address his PTSD symptoms and received support for grief and survivor's guilt. Over time, he was able to resume driving and cope with the emotional trauma associated with the accident.

Sir Mick Jagger, the iconic frontman of The Rolling Stones, is one of many celebrities to have been diagnosed with Post Traumatic Stress Disorder (PTSD). Jagger was left devastated by the passing of his long-term partner, L'Wren Scott, who took her own life in 2014. This traumatic event led to Jagger developing symptoms of PTSD such as nightmares, flashbacks, and severe anxiety surrounding death. He has now sought help from various mental health professionals in order to cope with his condition.

Harry, the Prince

Prince Harry, who is a member of the British royal family, has been candid about his struggles with PTSD. He struggled to deal emotionally with the impact of his experiences fighting in Afghanistan and serving in the British Army. One of the most difficult situations that contributed to his mental health concerns was the loss of his mother, Princess Diana when he was just twelve years old.

For a substantial length of time, Prince Harry buried his sentiments in favor of his royal obligations and military service. However, he hit his lowest point when he began experiencing uncontrollable sensations of wrath and anxiousness. He realized he needed assistance and went to treatment, and now he is a well-known voice in the push for mental health awareness. Prince Harry's experience has prompted a lot of individuals to seek therapy and communicate freely about their mental health difficulties.

Pop diva Gaga has just opened up about the agony of being sexually attacked when she was just 19 years old. She kept the tragedy to herself for years, but it had a terrible influence on her mental health. She maintained a highly successful singing career while having terrible mental pain, panic attacks, and physical signs of PTSD.

After a while, Lady Gaga went to therapy and started expressing her tale in public. By doing this, she has contributed to raising awareness of PTSD and sexual assault, especially with regard to how the latter can impact survivors long after the incident has taken place. Many people have been motivated by Lady Gaga's openness to talk about their own horrific experiences and obtain the care they seek.

Michael Phelps

The most decorated Olympian in history, Michael Phelps, has opened up about his difficulties with PTSD lately. His mental health worsened as a result of the weight of competing at the top level and putting in years of intensive training. After the 2012 London Olympics, in which he fell short of his ambitions, Phelps grappled with melancholy, anxiety, and pessimism.

He realized he had been battling with PTSD as a result of the strain of his sport and unsolved personal difficulties. Phelps started going to treatment and started talking frankly about his challenges with mental health. His tale has influenced athletes and others to put mental health first and receive therapy when they need it.

Theron Charlize

Oscar-winning actress Charlize Theron had PTSD as a result of a horrible childhood incident. Her father had threatened their lives, so when she was fifteen years old, her mother shot and murdered him in self-defense. This experience greatly impacted Charlize, and she battled with the emotional aftermath for a long period.

For a long period, Charlize kept the circumstances of her early life a secret, but gradually, she came out about how they had impacted her mental health. She suffered from extreme dread and flashbacks, which are frequent indications of post-traumatic stress disorder. She was able to handle her trauma with treatment, and she is now an advocate for mental health awareness. She has pushed others to obtain therapy and removed the stigma associated with PTSD by sharing her story.

The Ariana Grande

After a terrorist attack during her 2017 Manchester, England performance, pop singer and actress Ariana Grande acquired post-traumatic stress disorder (PTSD). The incident greatly upset Ariana and many others, leaving 22 dead and hundreds wounded. She suffered from anxiety, nightmares, and flashbacks to the horrible occurrence in the days that followed.

Since then, Ariana has made statements about how tough it was for her to heal emotionally from the event. She sought professional treatment and finally found coping skills for the recollections. Ariana has called attention to the emotional toll that catastrophic events may have, not just on the immediate victims but also on those who observe or are engaged in them indirectly, by sharing her personal experience.

It's important to remember that PTSD can affect anyone at any time - even celebrities like Sir Mick

Jagger are not immune to its effects. With the right support and treatment, those suffering from

PTSD can make progress toward recovery and live fulfilling lives.

CHAPTER 6
DEPRESSION AND ANXIETY DISORDER

In the complex tapestry of human existence, depression and anxiety disorders stand as pervasive and formidable threads, weaving their influence into the lives of countless individuals across the globe. These mental health challenges transcend age, gender, race, and socioeconomic status, affecting people from all walks of life. While their reach may be extensive, it is important to understand that depression and anxiety need not be life-defining; they can be confronted and conquered.

Depression and anxiety disorders are formidable adversaries that often manifest as invisible burdens, casting shadows over the inner landscapes of those who grapple with them. They are not exclusive to a particular demographic but cast a wide net, ensnaring children, adolescents, and adults alike. Regardless of one's background or station in life, these conditions can strike, making it imperative that we recognize and address them with empathy and understanding.

The roots of depression and anxiety are diverse and multifaceted. Physical illnesses, from chronic conditions that sap one's vitality to hormonal imbalances that disrupt emotional equilibrium, can serve as fertile ground for these disorders to take root. Traumatic life events, such as the loss of a loved one, the dissolution of a marriage, or exposure to violence, can create emotional wounds that fester, leading to these mental health challenges.

Relationship struggles, whether with friends, family, or romantic partners, can contribute to the weight of depression and anxiety. The complex dynamics of human connection can sometimes fuel feelings of isolation, rejection, or inadequacy, further exacerbating these conditions. Additionally, societal factors, such as financial stressors or the relentless pace of modern life, can pile on emotional burdens, amplifying the impact of these disorders.

However, it is essential to embrace the wisdom of Napoleon Hill's words: "The starting point of all achievement is desire." With knowledge, determination, and a willingness to confront these challenges head-on, individuals can embark on a journey of understanding and recovery. The path to healing begins with recognizing the existence of depression and anxiety, understanding their origins, and seeking the right support and treatment.

Education is a powerful tool in the battle against these mental health adversaries. Learning about the symptoms, causes, and available treatments for depression and anxiety can demystify these conditions, empowering individuals to take proactive steps toward their well-being. It is crucial to acknowledge that experiencing depression or anxiety is not a sign of weakness but rather a testament to one's resilience and capacity for growth.

Determination and a commitment to self-improvement are equally vital. Overcoming depression and anxiety often involves resilience-building strategies, including therapy, medication, lifestyle adjustments, and self-care practices. Therapy, such as cognitive-behavioural therapy (CBT) or mindfulness-based therapies, can equip individuals with coping skills and tools to manage the emotional turbulence that accompanies these conditions.

When prescribed and monitored by healthcare professionals, medication can help regulate brain chemistry and alleviate the intensity of symptoms. Lifestyle adjustments, such as maintaining a regular sleep schedule, engaging in physical activity, and practising stress management techniques, can significantly impact one's mood and overall well-being.

Self-care practices, too, are integral components of the healing journey. These can encompass everything from journaling and meditation to pursuing hobbies and engaging in meaningful social connections. Self-compassion is a cornerstone of self-care, reminding individuals that they deserve love, care, and understanding, especially in the face of mental health challenges.

In conclusion, depression and anxiety disorders are prevalent mental health issues that transcend boundaries and affect millions. They do not discriminate based on age, gender, race, or social status. Yet, they need not define our lives. Individuals can confront and conquer these formidable adversaries with the right knowledge, determination, and support. The journey may be challenging, but it is one of growth, resilience, and the reclamation of a fulfilling and purposeful life. As we strive for a more compassionate and understanding society, let us remember that the strength to overcome lies within each of us, waiting to be ignited by the desire for a brighter future.

TYPES OF DEPRESSION AND ANXIETY

There are several types of depression and anxiety disorders, each with its own set of symptoms and potential treatments. The most common forms include:

Major Depressive Disorder (MDD): MDD is characterized by persistent feelings of sadness, loss of interest in activities, changes in appetite or weight, sleep troubles, fatigue, difficulty concentrating, restlessness, suicidal thoughts, and other physical and emotional symptoms.

Generalized Anxiety Disorder (GAD): GAD involves excessive worry about a variety of topics that can last for at least six months. Symptoms include feeling on edge, irritability, difficulty concentrating, or sleeping well.

Panic Disorder: Panic disorder includes sudden episodes of fear or terror that come on without warning, often accompanied by physical symptoms like rapid heartbeat and chest pain.

Social Anxiety Disorder: This disorder involves fear of being embarrassed or judged in social situations, such as public speaking or meeting new people. It can lead to avoidance of certain activities and extreme self-consciousness.

SYMPTOMS OF DEPRESSION AND ANXIETY DISORDERS

Depression and anxiety disorders, often called the twin giants of mental health, are intricate conditions manifest in various forms, as unique as the individuals experiencing them. These disorders cast a shadow on millions of people's emotional and psychological well-being worldwide, and understanding their multifaceted nature is essential for effective recognition and support.

Depression, often described as a heavy, all-encompassing cloud that engulfs its victims, manifests through various symptoms. One of the most pervasive is the persistent feeling of sadness or emptiness. It's as if the colour has been drained from the world, and even the most joyous moments lose their vibrancy. This emotional weight is accompanied by debilitating fatigue, making even the simplest tasks feel like insurmountable mountains.

A telltale sign of depression is losing interest in activities that once brought pleasure and a sense of purpose. Hobbies and passions that used to light up an individual's life become dull and uninspiring. Concentration and decision-making become arduous, and simple choices can feel overwhelmingly complex.

Changes in appetite are common, with some experiencing an increase in food consumption while others lose their appetite entirely. Guilt and worthlessness often take root, plaguing the mind with self-critical thoughts that undermine self-esteem. The cumulative effect of these symptoms can lead to a pervasive sense of despair, further entrenching the depressive state.

Anxiety, on the other hand, is like a relentless storm within the mind and body. Excessive worry becomes a constant companion as individuals cannot shake off anxious thoughts about future uncertainties or potential dangers. Restlessness and irritability are pervasive, making it difficult to find calm or peace.

The physical toll of anxiety can be profound. Muscle tension can be so severe that it results in physical discomfort and pain. Sleep becomes elusive, with insomnia robbing individuals of the needed restorative rest. The racing heartbeat and shortness of breath are visceral manifestations of the body's heightened state of alertness, constantly primed for perceived threats.

One of the most insidious aspects of anxiety disorders is difficulty controlling worries. Anxious thoughts can spiral out of control, leading to a state of perpetual unease. These thoughts can be so overwhelming that they interfere with daily life, making concentrating on work or enjoying leisure activities challenging. The invisible chains of anxiety can trap individuals in a cycle of apprehension and fear.

It is crucial to acknowledge that those suffering from depression or anxiety may not outwardly display these symptoms. Many individuals are adept at concealing their emotional turmoil, even from close friends and family. The stigma surrounding mental health can lead people to wear masks of normalcy, hiding their inner struggles behind smiles and casual conversations. Therefore, someone can battle these conditions silently without any apparent physical indicators.

Recognizing and supporting individuals with depression and anxiety disorders requires sensitivity, empathy, and active listening. These conditions are not mere mood swings or passing worries; they are profound and often enduring struggles that affect every facet of a person's life. Encouraging open and non-judgmental conversations about mental health can help those in need feel more comfortable seeking help and ultimately finding the path to recovery.

In conclusion, depression and anxiety disorders are intricate conditions that manifest uniquely in each individual. Their symptoms can be both emotional and physical, and they often hide beneath a veneer of normalcy. Understanding the complexities of these disorders is essential to provide the support and compassion necessary for those suffering. By breaking down the stigma surrounding mental health and fostering an environment of empathy, society can play a vital role in helping individuals with depression and anxiety find their way toward healing and well-being.

CAUSES AND RISK FACTORS

Depression and anxiety disorders are multifaceted, and their causes can be as diverse as the individuals who experience them. A comprehensive understanding of the various factors contributing to these disorders is crucial for effective assessment, intervention, and support.

Physical health conditions can significantly impact an individual's mental well-being. Chronic pain and persistent fatigue, often associated with conditions like fibromyalgia or chronic fatigue syndrome, can wear down one's resilience and contribute to the onset of depression or anxiety. Hormonal imbalances, such as those occurring during menopause or as a result of thyroid dysfunction, can also influence mood and emotional stability. Likewise, deficiencies in essential vitamins and minerals, such as vitamin D or magnesium, can lead to emotional disturbances.

The thyroid, a crucial gland responsible for regulating metabolism, can profoundly influence mental health. Both hypothyroidism (underactive thyroid) and hyperthyroidism (overactive thyroid) can lead to mood swings, anxiety, and depressive symptoms. Sleep disturbances, whether due to sleep apnea, insomnia, or other sleep disorders, can further exacerbate these conditions by disrupting the body's natural rhythms.

Substance abuse is a complex issue that often goes hand in hand with depression and anxiety. The misuse of drugs or alcohol can provide temporary relief from emotional pain but ultimately worsen the underlying conditions. Substance abuse alters brain chemistry and creates a vicious cycle where individuals may rely on these substances to cope with their emotional distress.

Traumatic life events can act as potent triggers for depression and anxiety. The death of a loved one, the dissolution of a marriage through divorce, the loss of employment, or experiencing violence and abuse can all shatter an individual's sense of security and stability. Natural disasters like hurricanes, earthquakes, or wildfires can have profound and lasting psychological effects, often leading to post-traumatic stress disorder (PTSD). Even the seemingly mundane, like moving to a new city, can disrupt one's life and trigger these disorders.

Genetic predisposition plays a pivotal role in the development of depression and anxiety. Research has shown that individuals with a family history of these disorders are more vulnerable to experiencing them. While specific genes associated with depression and anxiety have yet to be definitively identified, it is clear that genetic factors interact with environmental influences to shape an individual's susceptibility.

Certain personality traits can also increase the risk of developing these disorders. Perfectionism, for instance, can lead to relentless self-criticism and an unattainable quest for flawlessness, setting the stage for depression and anxiety to take root. Additionally, people with highly sensitive or introverted temperaments may be more prone to experiencing emotional distress in response to life's challenges.

Childhood experiences, particularly those involving abuse or neglect, can leave deep emotional scars that persist into adulthood. Individuals who have endured trauma during their formative years may carry the emotional burden. The residual effects of childhood abuse can manifest as depression and anxiety, often compounded by feelings of shame and self-blame.

Environmental factors also play a significant role in developing depression and anxiety. Major life changes, such as starting college, getting married, or becoming a parent, can bring about profound shifts in one's routine and responsibilities. While often positive, these transitions can also be accompanied by increased stress and anxiety as individuals navigate new challenges and responsibilities.

The presence or absence of social support is a critical environmental factor. Isolation and a lack of close relationships can amplify feelings of loneliness and despair, making it more difficult to cope with life's trials. Financial stressors, such as job loss or overwhelming debt, can exacerbate hopelessness and anxiety, compounding the burden.

Self-esteem, or the lack thereof, significantly influences mental health. Individuals with low selfesteem may be more susceptible to depression and anxiety, as they may internalize negative experiences and beliefs about their self-worth. Additionally, the pervasive influence of social media and the constant comparison to others can contribute to feelings of inadequacy and fuel anxiety.

In conclusion, depression and anxiety disorders are not born from a single cause but rather arise from a complex interplay of physical, genetic, environmental, and psychological factors.

Understanding this intricate web of influences is essential for healthcare professionals and loved ones seeking to support those affected by these conditions. By recognizing the diverse range of factors that can contribute to depression and anxiety, we can develop more comprehensive strategies for prevention, intervention, and recovery, ultimately offering hope and relief to those who suffer.

TREATING DEPRESSION AND ANXIETY DISORDERS

Fortunately, depression and anxiety disorders can be treated in a variety of ways. The type of treatment used will depend on the individual's symptoms and needs – for instance, some people may benefit from talk therapy alone while others might need medication as well.

Psychotherapy is one of the most effective ways to treat depression and anxiety. Cognitive Behavioral Therapy (CBT) has been studied extensively as a leading psychotherapeutic approach for addressing these issues. CBT helps individuals identify unhealthy thought patterns and behaviors, and replace them with healthier ones.

In CBT, individuals learn specific skills they can use to manage their symptoms in day-to-day life, such as identifying triggers that precede anxiety or depressive episodes and learning techniques to cope with these episodes when they occur. Individuals can also learn relaxation techniques such as deep breathing or progressive muscle relaxation which can be useful in managing stress levels or calming an anxious mind.

CBT often includes exposure exercises where individuals are gradually exposed to situations that make them feel anxious or depressed in order to reduce their emotional reactivity over time. For example, if someone has a social anxiety disorder (SAD), they may participate in gradual exposure activities such as role-playing conversations with others or attending increasingly larger gatherings until they no longer experience extreme discomfort when engaging in social activities.

CBT does not simply focus on managing symptoms; it addresses underlying causes of depression and anxiety by targeting dysfunctional thoughts and beliefs about oneself, others, and the world around us. These dysfunctional beliefs are called "schemas" and CBT helps clients challenge these schemas so that more realistic thoughts can take their place. This allows individuals to see themselves in a more positive light while being better able to cope with negative emotions when they arise.

Medication may be prescribed in conjunction with psychotherapy or on its own. Commonly used antidepressants are selective serotonin reuptake inhibitors (SSRIs) and serotonin-norepinephrine reuptake inhibitors (SNRIs). It is important to note that it can take several weeks for an individual to experience the full effects of antidepressant medication, so patience is required when starting a new treatment regimen.

Other medications such as benzodiazepines may be prescribed for short-term relief of anxiety symptoms. Benzodiazepines, however, are not a long-term solution as they can be habit-forming and have potential side effects. It is important to discuss any medication with a doctor before taking it in order to ensure the safest course of treatment possible.

Treatments such as electroconvulsive therapy (ECT) have also been proven effective for severe cases of depression. In ECT, electrical pulses are applied to the brain in order to induce a seizure which then temporarily alters levels of neurotransmitters associated with mood regulation.

Other treatments for depression and anxiety may include lifestyle changes such as getting regular exercise and sufficient sleep, maintaining social support networks, practicing mindfulness, eating healthy foods, and avoiding alcohol and drugs. Additionally, light therapy has been shown to help improve symptoms of seasonal affective disorder (SAD) by providing exposure to artificial bright light.

AN ACCOUNT OF A FEW PEOPLE WHO HAD DEPRESSION AND ANXIETY DISORDERS

There is a celebrity that many admire for their success in Hollywood, openness about struggling with depression and anxiety, as well as their bravery. Growing up he experienced deep feelings of shame and low self-esteem. At 15 years old, he made one of the bravest decisions of his life; he saved his mother from a suicide attempt by taking her to rehab.

Years later, he opened up about the depression he experienced throughout his life and encouraged people not to be afraid to open up and get help if necessary. This celebrity is now an inspiring example of how it is possible to overcome depression and anxiety through hard work and resilience.

In an interview with Express, a British newspaper, he said that "Struggle and pain are real". On Twitter, he wrote "Depression never discriminates" and encouraged people not to be afraid to open up and get help if necessary.

Who is this celebrity? It's Dwayne Johnson, also known as The Rock.

J.K. Rowling is a perfect example of how creativity and imagination can be used to overcome depression. Despite feeling despair while writing her magical Harry Potter series, Rowling was able to use her experiences of darkness to create the beloved characters and stories that we know today. In her own words, "Rock bottom became the solid foundation on which I rebuilt my life."

Rowling has opened up about her struggles with depression over the years, often encouraging others to seek help if they need it. In 2010, she told Oprah Winfrey that talking about depression is important because it can make people feel less alone. She also believes that it is important to remember that "it is possible to come back from even the darkest of places".

There was an actor, renowned for his wit and charisma on the silver screen. His comedic performances in movies such as Good Will Hunting and Mrs. Doubtfire put him firmly in the hearts of millions around the world. However, beneath his successful career lay a deep struggle with depression that even those closest to him were unaware of.

In 2006, this actor opened up about his experience with depression to NPR's Terry Gross. He described what it was like living with two completely different sides to himself; one full of joy and energy while the other felt empty and bleak. He also shared how difficult it was to maintain such an extreme exchange between these two states and how he would often use substances and alcohol as a temporary escape from the darkness.

These struggles eventually took a toll on this actor who, in 2014, tragically committed suicide. In the wake of his death, many people around the world were left stunned and saddened by the loss of an icon. It has also sparked conversations about depression, raising awareness for those struggling with mental health issues to seek help and support from loved ones or professionals if needed.

Although his life was cut short, the legacy of Robin Williams lives on in his films and comedy specials that will continue to make us laugh for years to come. His story serves as a reminder that no matter how powerful we may seem on the outside, everyone is susceptible to bouts of anxiety and depression something that should be taken seriously and addressed with care.

His passing left a void in the hearts of millions, but his name will continue to be remembered as an icon who touched us all - Robin Williams.

Ellen DeGeneres is a beloved figure in the United States and beyond. Known for her hit TV show The Ellen DeGeneres Show since 2003, she has won countless awards and honors as a comedian, actress, writer, producer, and LGBTQ+ rights activist.

However, this was not always the case - in 1997 when Ellen publicly came out as a lesbian, it caused an immense stir of controversy within Hollywood and society alike. As a result of this decision, the show faced extreme bullying from audiences and eventually got canceled after one season. This pushed Ellen into a deep depression that lasted several years.

Despite this, Ellen was determined to overcome her depression and persevere. With the help of therapy, meditation, exercise, and antidepressants, she slowly began to feel more hopeful about her future. Her resilience paid off when in 2003 Ellen returned to TV with The Ellen DeGeneres Show which quickly became a hit.

We all know that person who rose to fame with their debut album in 2010, selling over 20 million albums and singles worldwide. But few of us know the real story behind her success; the personal struggles she overcame to get there.

This person battled anxiety and depression during the early years of her career, weighed down by the pressures of performing and a lack of self-confidence. To cope, she tried desperately to cover her face with a pillow when out in public so that nobody could see the panic attacks she was experiencing.

But she was determined to overcome her mental health issues and turned to songwriting as a way of expressing her emotions. She also practiced meditation and mindfulness, helping to improve her self-confidence and reduce the intensity of her anxiety attacks.

The person we are talking about is Ellie Goulding – a multi-platinum artist who is also well known for her work as an advocate for mental health awareness. Through her determination to face her fears and come out stronger than before, she has become an inspiring role model for all of us.

Let's talk about Abraham Lincoln? Abraham Lincoln, the 16th president of the United States, is widely considered one of the finest leaders in American history. His ability to lead the country during the Civil War and abolish slavery is a credit to his strength, vision, and dedication. However, beneath the appearance of a strong and uncompromising leader was a man who endured severe personal challenges. Lincoln fought with what we now understand as severe depression for most of his life, a problem that added complexity to his incredible journey.

Lincoln's battle with depression, frequently referred to as "melancholy" during his period, began long before he entered politics. Born into a low-income family in Kentucky in 1809, Lincoln had a rough childhood filled with loss and sorrow. His mother died when he was just nine years old, and this early bereavement had a great influence on him. Lincoln was a sensitive boy, and the sadness from losing his mother would linger with him for the rest of his life. As a young man, Lincoln often felt a great feeling of melancholy and solitude. He struggled to find his place in the world, and many who knew him remarked on his tendency to lapse into bouts of extreme depression. Lincoln's legal partner and biographer, William Herndon, reportedly described him as a guy who was "inexpressibly sad" and prone to mood swings. Even before he became president, Lincoln's emotional troubles were clear to those closest to him.

Lincoln also endured personal traumas that aggravated his mental health difficulties. His first love, Ann Rutledge, died when she was barely 22 years old, leaving Lincoln distraught. Her death was a severe blow, and many believe it precipitated one of his worst depression spells. In the wake of her demise, Lincoln sank into a state of depression, withdrawing from social engagements and pondering his mortality. He talked about his anguish in letters to pals, describing sentiments of hopelessness and helplessness.

Despite these limitations, Lincoln found purpose and meaning in his job. His drive and desire to make a difference in the world helped him manage his sadness, albeit it was always lurking under the surface. Lincoln's political career took off when he was elected to the Illinois State Legislature in 1834, and he continued to ascend through the levels of American politics, finally becoming president in 1860. However, even during his most prosperous years, Lincoln's sadness lingered. The stresses of the presidency, along with the personal losses he faced, compounded his emotional issues. The Civil War, which took the lives of hundreds of thousands of Americans, weighed hard on Lincoln's conscience. He felt personally responsible for the lives lost, and the great strain of governing a divided nation took a toll on his mental health.

Lincoln's wife, Mary Todd Lincoln, also suffered from mental health concerns, notably following the loss of their son, Willie, in 1862. Willie's death was a shattering blow to both Lincoln and his wife, and it put the president into a profound despair. During this era, Lincoln was often observed to be in intense grief. Friends and coworkers remarked that he would sit alone for hours, looking into the distance, overcome by loss and misery. Despite his anguish, Lincoln continued to lead the nation with unyielding conviction. Many historians feel that his struggles with sadness provided him with a unique perspective on human suffering and helped him acquire a great sense of empathy for others. This sensitivity enabled him to connect with people on a fundamental level, which was vital during a moment of national crisis. Lincoln's capacity to persist through personal suffering while leading the country through its worst days is one of the reasons he is hailed as one of America's greatest presidents.

Lincoln's coping techniques for dealing with depression were not always healthy by today's standards. He often suppressed his feelings, believing that it was his job as a leader to put the needs of the country ahead of his well-being. He seldom sought care for his mental health, as mental illness was largely stigmatized during the 19th century. Instead, he relied on his job, his sense of responsibility, and his religion to bring him through the toughest days of his life.

One way Lincoln controlled his sadness was through comedy. He was noted for his wit and storytelling ability, frequently employing comedy to distract attention from his psychological troubles. His jokes and tales provided him with a momentary reprieve from the weight of his obligations and the grief that frequently overtook him. Humor helped Lincoln connect with people and retain a feeling of normalcy, even when he was fighting inside.

Lincoln also sought refuge in books, particularly poetry. He was an enthusiastic reader and often turned to the writings of Shakespeare and the Bible for solace during tough times. One of his favorite poems, "Mortality" by William Knox, showed his dismal vision of life and death. The poem, which speaks of the fleeting essence of human existence, is strongly connected with Lincoln and echoes his ideas about mortality.

In addition to comedy and literature, Lincoln found strength in his sense of purpose. He believed profoundly in the purpose of maintaining the Union and eradicating slavery, and this feeling of responsibility helped him stay focused on his aims, even when his despair made it impossible to continue. His desire to lead the nation through the Civil War motivated him to push through the darkest circumstances of his life.

Lincoln's despair, while a cause of immense personal sorrow, may have also contributed to his success as a leader. His experiences with misery and hopelessness gave him a greater awareness of human suffering, which made him more sympathetic and sensitive toward others. This sensitivity was visible in his lectures and writings, where he constantly spoke of the need for healing and reconciliation. For example, in his second inaugural address, delivered only weeks before his assassination, Lincoln spoke of the necessity for "malice toward none" and "charity for all" as the nation sought to rebuild after the Civil War. His statements revealed a deep appreciation of the grief and suffering that the war had created, both for the troops on the battlefield and the families at home. Lincoln's capacity to sympathize with the hardships of others helped him connect with the American people during a period of enormous adversity.

Lincoln's despair also may have contributed to his perseverance. Despite confronting great personal and professional hardships, he never gave up on his objective to maintain the Union and eradicate slavery. His capacity to persist despite hardship is one of the distinguishing features of his administration. Even when the war looked unwinnable and his personal life was fraught with sorrow, Lincoln remained constant in his dedication to his nation.

Historians have long questioned the significance that Lincoln's mental health had in establishing his leadership style. Some feel that his sadness made him more careful and analytical in his decision-making, while others claim that it pushed him to take bold and decisive action when necessary. Regardless of how his melancholy affected his leadership, there is little doubt that Lincoln's ability to overcome his troubles while leading the country through its most arduous era is a monument to his grit and character.

Abraham Lincoln's struggle with depression is a significant aspect of his legacy, as it reveals the intricacies of his character and the problems he endured behind the scenes. While his public image was one of power and drive, his private life was plagued by great melancholy and mental suffering. Yet, despite these hurdles, Lincoln was able to accomplish greatness and leave a lasting impression on the world.

In recent years, Lincoln's difficulties with mental health have become a subject of growing curiosity, particularly as the stigma around mental illness has begun to disappear. His tale serves as a reminder that even the most successful and accomplished persons can encounter mental health issues. It also underscores the need to seek help and find healthy methods to cope with emotional problems.

Lincoln's life proves that mental health challenges do not determine a person's value or restrict their potential. His ability to endure depression while leading the country through its most difficult moment is a monument to his tenacity, grit, and commitment. Today, his tale continues to inspire individuals who endure similar circumstances, reminding them that it is possible to accomplish greatness, even in the face of severe personal sorrow.

Depression and anxiety can be very difficult to manage, but with the right treatment plan and support, individuals can learn to live a meaningful life despite these conditions. It is important to remember that each person's journey toward recovery is unique, so it is essential to find the approach that works best for you. Professional help from therapists or psychiatrists may be beneficial if self-help techniques are not enough. With the right combination of medication, psychotherapy, and lifestyle changes, most people can lead fulfilling lives free from depression and anxiety.

CHAPTER 7
BIPOLAR DISORDER

Bipolar Disorder, a formidable and often misunderstood mental health condition, touches the lives of millions across the globe, leaving a profound impact on individuals and their loved ones. This complex disorder is marked by dramatic and fluctuating mood, energy levels, and behaviour shifts, which can be so extreme that they disrupt the fabric of everyday life.

At the heart of Bipolar Disorder are two distinct phases: manic or hypomanic episodes and depressive episodes. These episodes can span varying durations, from days to months, and their intensity can vary widely from person to person.

Mania is characterized by heightened energy, joy, and vitality that can border on euphoria. Individuals experiencing a manic episode often display racing thoughts, rapid speech, and an intense desire to engage in pleasurable activities, often to excess. These behaviours can include impulsive spending sprees, risky sexual behaviour, or taking on ambitious projects without consideration of the consequences.

Hypomania, a milder form of mania, shares many of these characteristics but to a lesser degree. While it may not result in the same level of impairment or recklessness as a full-blown manic episode, hypomania can still disrupt one's life and relationships. It's essential to recognize that periods of mania or hypomania, while often characterized by invincibility, can lead to serious consequences, such as financial ruin, damaged relationships, or legal issues.

Conversely, depressive episodes in Bipolar Disorder bring forth a starkly contrasting emotional landscape. These periods are characterized by persistent sadness, hopelessness, and despair. Energy levels plummet, and individuals may struggle to find motivation for the simplest tasks.

Sleep disturbances, appetite changes, and profound fatigue become the norm.

Depressive episodes can be just as debilitating as manic or hypomanic ones, if not more so. The emotional pain can be excruciating, and thoughts of self-harm or suicide may intrude upon the mind. It's crucial to emphasize that Bipolar Disorder is not simply a matter of experiencing mood swings; it encompasses profound and sustained shifts in mood and energy that are beyond the control of the individual.

While Bipolar Disorder is not curable, effective treatments are available to manage its symptoms and help individuals lead fulfilling lives. Medication, such as mood stabilizers, antipsychotics, or antidepressants, is often prescribed to help regulate mood swings and manage symptoms. Psychotherapy, particularly cognitive-behavioral therapy (CBT), can provide individuals with coping strategies and tools to navigate the emotional challenges of Bipolar Disorder.

Lifestyle modifications are also an integral part of managing Bipolar Disorder. Maintaining a stable routine that includes regular sleep patterns, a balanced diet, exercise, and stress management techniques can help minimize the frequency and severity of mood episodes. Individuals with Bipolar Disorder need to work closely with mental health professionals to develop a personalized treatment plan tailored to their unique needs and experiences.

The journey to managing Bipolar Disorder can be challenging, but individuals do not need to undertake it alone. A robust support system, including friends, family, and support groups, can play a vital role in helping those with Bipolar Disorder cope with their condition and navigate the ups and downs of their emotional landscape.

It's also essential to reduce the stigma and misconceptions surrounding Bipolar Disorder and mental health. This disorder is not a reflection of weakness or a character flaw. Rather, a complex interplay of genetic, biochemical, and environmental factors contributes to its development.

DIFFERENT TYPES OF BIPOLAR DISORDER

Bipolar disorder is a complex and impactful mental illness that disrupts the lives of millions of people worldwide. This condition is characterized by profound and often dramatic shifts in mood, energy levels, activity patterns, and the ability to perform daily tasks. Throughout history, bipolar disorder has been known by various names, such as manic depression, cyclothymic disorder, hyperthymic disorder, and manic-depressive illness, underscoring its long-standing recognition and study.

The most prevalent form of bipolar disorder is Bipolar I Disorder. Individuals diagnosed with this subtype experience one or more episodes of mania or hypomania, a less severe form of mania interspersed with episodes of depression. During manic phases, individuals often exhibit extraordinary productivity and boundless energy, but reckless behaviours, impulsivity, and poor decision-making can also mark these periods. In stark contrast, depressive episodes in Bipolar I Disorder can render individuals incapable of engaging in everyday activities, leaving them mired in profound sadness and hopelessness.

Bipolar II Disorder is another distinct subtype of the condition, characterized by alternating episodes of hypomania and major depression. Unlike Bipolar I Disorder, Bipolar II does not involve full-blown manic episodes but rather milder hypomanic states. People with Bipolar II Disorder may also experience more frequent and prolonged depressive episodes than their Bipolar I counterparts, making it a unique presentation.

Cyclothymic disorder represents a chronic and less severe form of bipolar disorder. Individuals with this subtype cycle between hypomanic and depressive states over a minimum of two years. These cycles typically do not meet the criteria for major depression or full-blown mania, but they can still significantly disrupt an individual's life. Although the episodes of cyclothymic disorder are generally less severe, their chronic nature can create ongoing challenges.

Rapid-cycling bipolar disorder is a specialized condition where individuals endure four or more mood episodes within twelve months. This rapid cycling between mania, hypomania, and depression can be especially challenging to manage and treat, necessitating a tailored approach to treatment.

Thankfully, several effective treatment options are available for individuals grappling with bipolar disorder. These include mood stabilizers, antipsychotics, and atypical antidepressants, which can help stabilize mood swings. Psychotherapy is vital in helping individuals manage their symptoms, gain insight into their condition, and develop coping strategies. Self-help techniques, lifestyle modifications, and alternative therapies contribute to comprehensive treatment plans. The management of bipolar disorder is highly individualized, and finding the right combination of treatments is essential to enable those affected to lead fulfilling and productive lives despite the challenges posed by this complex mental illness.

SYMPTOMS AND DIAGNOSIS

Bipolar Disorder is a complex mental health condition characterized by marked mood, energy levels, and behaviour fluctuations. These mood swings are divided into two primary states: manic and depressive episodes, each with distinct symptoms.

- **MANIC EPISODES:**

During manic episodes, individuals often experience a heightened sense of euphoria or, in some cases, intense irritability. Their energy levels surge to unprecedented heights, and they engage in excessive activity. This often results in a decreased need for sleep, and they may go without rest for extended periods. Their speech becomes rapid and expansive, filled with racing thoughts that can be challenging to follow. Impulsive behaviours are common during manic episodes, including extravagant spending sprees, risky sexual encounters, or engaging in activities with potentially harmful consequences.

- **DEPRESSIVE EPISODES:**

In contrast, depressive episodes bring about a profound sense of sadness, despair, or hopelessness. Individuals may lose interest in activities they once found enjoyable and pleasurable. Changes in eating habits manifest, with some individuals experiencing overeating and weight gain, while others may lose their appetite and suffer from significant weight loss. Social withdrawal becomes prevalent as individuals isolate themselves from social interactions and conversations. Sleep disturbances are common, with some experiencing insomnia and others oversleeping. Concentration and focus are impaired, making even simple tasks feel overwhelming. A pervasive fatigue often accompanies depressive episodes, leaving individuals drained and exhausted.

Diagnosing Bipolar Disorder is a comprehensive process that requires careful evaluation by a healthcare professional. It typically commences with a physical examination and a thorough medical history review to eliminate other potential causes of the symptoms, such as medical conditions or medications.

The diagnostic criteria outlined in the DSM-5 (Diagnostic and Statistical Manual of Mental Disorders) are crucial in assessing Bipolar Disorder. This manual delineates specific criteria for various types of bipolar disorder, ensuring a standardized and accurate assessment. To receive a diagnosis of bipolar disorder, an individual must have experienced at least one manic or hypomanic episode, along with severe depression that significantly interferes with their daily life. These criteria help ensure that individuals receive the appropriate diagnosis and treatment, as managing Bipolar Disorder often necessitates tailored approaches to address both manic and depressive phases of the condition.

CAUSES AND RISK FACTORS

Bipolar disorder is a complex mental illness, and while its exact cause remains elusive, extensive research has shed light on several factors that are believed to contribute to its development. These factors encompass biological and environmental influences and interplay in intricate ways to give rise to this challenging condition.

- **GENETICS:**

Genetics is widely regarded as one of the primary risk factors for bipolar disorder. Research has shown that individuals with a family history of bipolar disorder are at a significantly higher risk of developing the condition. This genetic predisposition suggests that specific gene variants or combinations may make some individuals more susceptible to bipolar disorder than others. While genetics play a crucial role, it is important to note that not everyone with a family history of bipolar disorder will develop the condition, indicating that other factors are also at play.

- **BIOLOGICAL FACTORS:**

Within biology, researchers have identified various neurochemical and structural brain differences in individuals with bipolar disorder. Imbalances in neurotransmitters like serotonin, dopamine, and norepinephrine are thought to contribute to mood disturbances. Additionally, structural changes in specific brain regions associated with emotional regulation and impulse control have been observed in individuals with bipolar disorder. These biological factors suggest a neurobiological basis for the disorder, although their precise role in its development is still being explored.

- **ENVIRONMENTAL FACTORS:**

Environmental stressors can significantly impact the onset and course of bipolar disorder. Physical or emotional trauma, such as childhood abuse or neglect, can increase an individual's vulnerability to the disorder. Traumatic experiences may act as triggers that bring latent genetic predispositions to the forefront. Stressful life events, such as major life changes or chronic stress, can also contribute to the development of bipolar disorder or exacerbate its symptoms.

- **SUBSTANCE USE:**

Substance abuse, including alcohol and drug use, is recognized as a significant factor that can worsen existing bipolar symptoms and contribute to the onset of manic episodes. Substances like stimulants or alcohol can induce manic-like symptoms, leading to a vicious cycle of mood instability and impaired judgment. Individuals with bipolar disorder must avoid substance use, as it can complicate treatment efforts and exacerbate the challenges associated with the condition.

The development of bipolar disorder is believed to be influenced by a complex interplay of genetic, biological, and environmental factors. While genetics predispose some individuals to the disorder, environmental stressors and substance use can trigger or worsen symptoms. Understanding these factors is vital for early intervention and effective management of bipolar disorder, as it underscores the importance of comprehensive treatment approaches that address the condition's biological and psychosocial aspects.

MANAGING BIPOLAR DISORDER

Managing the symptoms of bipolar disorder is a lifelong process that requires ongoing effort and commitment. Treatment generally involves medications, psychotherapy, lifestyle changes, and self-help strategies. The goal of treatment is to reduce symptoms and prevent future episodes; however, it can take some time to find the right combination of treatments that works for an individual.

Medication is typically the first line of defense against bipolar disorder. Typically, mood stabilizers are used to help reduce manic episodes and are often coupled with other medications such as antipsychotics or antidepressants to reduce depressive symptoms. It's important to remember that all medications come with potential side effects, so it's important to speak with your doctor regularly about any side effects that you are experiencing.

In addition to medications, psychotherapy is an important part of managing bipolar disorder. Cognitive Behavioral Therapy (CBT) is a type of therapy that can help individuals understand the patterns in their thinking and behavior, identify triggers for manic episodes, and develop healthy coping strategies to better manage their symptoms. Other types of therapies such as Interpersonal Therapy (IPT) and Dialectical Behavior Therapy (DBT) may also be beneficial for some individuals.

Lifestyle changes can also play an important role in managing bipolar disorder. It's important to have regular routines with set times for sleeping, eating, and exercising; engage in activities that bring joy and reduce stress; limit or avoid substances; and practice relaxation techniques such as yoga, meditation, or deep breathing. Additionally, developing a strong support system of family and friends can be beneficial for managing symptoms.

Finally, self-help strategies can help individuals better manage their bipolar disorder. This includes keeping a mood journal to track changes in moods and behavior; setting realistic goals; identifying triggers that may lead to manic episodes; learning how to recognize early warning signs of an episode; engaging in healthy activities such as walking or reading; joining support groups that provide education and emotional support from peers living with bipolar disorder; and taking steps to build relationships with others.

Managing bipolar disorder is a complex process that requires ongoing effort and commitment from both the individual and the healthcare team. With the right combination of treatment, lifestyle changes, and strategies for self-care, it is possible to lead a fulfilling life and overcome the challenges of bipolar disorder.

The most important thing to remember is that you are not alone in managing your bipolar disorder and there are resources available to support you on this journey.

AN ACCOUNT OF A FEW PEOPLE WHO HAD BIPOLAR DISORDER

A man was photographed begging for money at a Dallas gas station in 2020. Little did anyone know, but the destitute figure was actually a former NBA player who had been struggling with bipolar disorder for years. He had come to terms with his mental health and decided to put up a fight; however, he felt powerless against the pressure of being successful.

Desperate, he was picked up from the same gas station by Mark Cuban, the owner of the Dallas Mavericks, who wanted to help him get back on his feet. It was the start of a spiritual journey towards reclaiming normalcy and accepting his mental health struggles as they came.

He eventually started getting involved in charity work and advocating more awareness about bipolar disorder. In interviews, he shared stories of how he found strength in himself and others while battling the disorder over the years. His story was inspiring because of its message of resilience and hope.

When all seemed lost, this brave man never gave up - his name is Delonte West. He has become a beacon of light for those who are struggling with bipolar disorder, reminding us to take care of our mental well-being and never give up in the face of adversity. He encourages all of us to seek help, stay positive and fight against the odds.

Delonte West is an inspirational figure who has fought through his battle with bipolar disorder and emerged as a role model for us all. His story of strength is proof that no matter how dark our mental health might seem, there is always hope for recovery.

The two illnesses that are most often misdiagnosed are bipolar disorder and schizophrenia. When in a dilemma, these conditions change a person's train of thought, emotions, and behaviour, which generally complicates the performance of day-to-day tasks. These diseases have, nevertheless, not totally hindered many afflicted people from enjoying highly productive and fulfilling lives. They show how people with mental health conditions have tested perseverance, individualism and determination. Some of the most famous are John Nash, Mariah Carey, Jean-Claude Van Damme and Kanye West. All the people who gave their testimonials helped in increasing awareness of these disorders. These stories help us understand that mental illness is not who you are or what you can become.

Speaking of Kanye West first. In popular culture and fashion and music in particular, Kanye is quite influential. There is no doubt that he changed hip-hop music, and there is no better way to innovate. Yet, the public image that Kanye has cultivated for a long time has been dubious for as long as he has ranted and raved during his most passionate performances. Kanye further revealed that he was diagnosed with bipolar illness in 2018. It was crucial for him and for how the audience perceived his acts, too.

Wide fluctuations in mood characterize bipolar disease. Bi-polar is usually characterized by a high surge of energy and a feeling of happiness, power and accomplishments for some period, followed by a period of deep and severe hose. In public life, in which the media has documented his rants and bizarre behaviour, Kanye has often shown symptoms of manic episodes.

In one way or another, the public may bend it in a way that might lead to criticism or even mockery of the occurrences. However, Kanye has not been shy about admitting that some of his most creative pieces have their roots in his manias. Some of his most well-known songs and fashion creations are the result of his prolific mind, his voracious appetite, and his manic energy.

However, conflict with the management of the depressed stages is a problem associated with this. Like many other bipolar people, Kanye, at times, could hardly stand to be alive and wished to sleep forever; he felt severe and utter sadness. It can be tiring for him and anyone nearby when he has these mood swings. Kanye has spoken in interviews about how hard it is to nurture relationships and make choices during these periods. He has also spoken about discrimination that he has faced whenever he speaks about mental health as a black man. Due to the fact that mental illness has not been embraced in many countries, Kanye's being very open has made people with such issues discuss the problems in various countries.

Everyone can get a mental disorder regardless of fame. Such a story of Kanye is a sad example. It also focuses on how important it is to seek help, whether through a therapist, through medication, or through talking about mental health with people. On this platform, Kanye has encouraged people to make mental health the most important priority and to be more sensitive to people who are challenged.

Mariah Carey is another celebrity whose life has illuminated the problem of mental health issues. A true phenomenon in her genre, Mariah has composed, sung and arranged songs that topped the charts and showed off her remarkable vocal range. But all that glitters during those days was not gold, and it appeared there was more to Mariah than fame and glamour, the reality being that Mariah indeed had bipolar problems. It was in December 2018 that Mariah came out to the public to announce that she was a sufferer of bipolar II illness, which involves the worst forms of depressive episodes and relatively lesser incidences of hypomania. Kanye and Mariah remained in silence for years, struggling to seek professional help because seeking help could of meant losing their jobs.

Mariah has spoken about the terror she felt around her diagnosis. Early in the new millennium, mental health was still considered taboo, particularly in the entertainment industry, where there was constant pressure to project perfection. Mariah kept her diagnosis a secret for a while because she didn't want the world to believe she was unstable or inadequate. Rather, she concentrated on her career, writing songs and touring the globe. But finally, the cost of untreated mental illness became intolerable. She had extreme mood swings and tired spells that made it difficult for her to carry out her personal and professional obligations.

Mariah didn't start to control her life and manage her symptoms until she asked for assistance. She gained knowledge about navigating the ups and downs of bipolar disease through treatment and medication. Although it was difficult, Mariah felt that sharing her story about her mental health journey was a crucial first step. She has subsequently become a champion for mental health awareness, particularly for women who, like her, may feel compelled to keep up appearances while battling inwardly.

Mariah's narrative is important because it demonstrates that people with seemingly perfect lives may struggle with mental health issues. Her story serves as a reminder that getting care for a mental illness is not anything to be embarrassed by and that doing so may result in a more balanced and fulfilled existence.

Many people have found strength in Mariah's voice, both physically and figuratively, and her choice to be transparent about her disease has surely made others feel less alone in their challenges.

Another famous example is the Belgian actor and martial artist Jean-Claude Van Damme, who had to face the most terrible problems with mental health issues. These action films, such as Bloodsport and Kickboxer starred the famous actor. As much as he hid his intellectual and emotional side because of the body-building type cast, Van Damme had a severe mental disorder. He did not get a bipolar illness diagnosis until later in his career, which gave a reason for years of fluctuations and personal problems in his behaviour.

Van Damme has not hidden his bipolar affair, which is a kind of mental illness, from his fans. He explained that during these highs, he felt as though he could do no wrong; due to this, during his manic episodes, he would do things that he knew were wrong and place himself in danger. I believe that Van Damme would have a strong want to push himself to the absolute limit during such times, both psychologically and physically. Though this helped him to obtain success in his acting and his martial arts career, this led to emotional pain, which included alcoholism and strained family relations.

It was also bowels to entertain deep lows, as was with Van Damme, many who have bipolar illness. He would sometimes be down, and he could not seem to interact with people in society, and he felt so lonely from the inside. He did not understand how to deal with this randomly changing mood for several days, which is why his illness remained undiagnosed. He did not begin to understand his disease and its management until he looked for professional help. The tale of Van Damme is one of perseverance. He has talked about how receiving therapy and medicine has helped him achieve stability. He is still employed in the film business, but he is more aware of his mental health now. It has been crucial that he be open about his bipolar illness, particularly in a place like Hollywood, where mental health concerns are sometimes concealed beneath the gloss and glamour. Van Damme's tale illustrates that even in the most physically demanding careers, mental wellness is equally as vital as physical fitness.

Schizophrenia is another condition that people with bipolar disorder are often diagnosed wrongly together with the original disease. Chronic schizophrenia is a major mental disorder that affects a person's thought processes, emotions, and behaviours. Patients with this disease may then have to face delusions, suffer from hallucinations, as well as have problems with logical thinking. Still, most of them, if properly taken care of and provided for, can lead normal, productive lives. Among the most famous examples, one can list John Nash, a brilliant mathematician featured in the film A Beautiful Mind.

John Nash was only in his early 30s when symptoms indicative of schizophrenia surfaced and sent him plummeting to oblivion. He had paranoid delusions, and for a while, it looked as though his career might falter because of the illness. But Nash managed to keep his disease in check using medication, counselling and support from his family. Nonetheless, Nash never relented from giving significant input to mathematics, especially in the field of game theory. He was a true economic prophet, and in 1994, he was awarded the Nobel Prize in Economics for his work, which proved his intelligence and persistence.

That is why Nash's story is quite powerful, helping to emphasize that a person's mental disorder does not mean they are the disorder themselves. With such a disease, under particular circumstances, it is quite achievable to be successful. Another issue that has been learned from Nash's life is the importance of support networks, which can come from friends, family or mental health specialists. Schizophrenic patients can regulate their signs and continue with their leisure activities if they gain the right support.

Mental health has been an issue of great concern globally, and the way individuals communicate about their difficulties has had a huge influence on communities. For so long, there has been a stigma around mental health, but more people, especially celebrities, are coming out about their personal experiences. They are teaching us that even with mental health difficulties, one can still do remarkable things. This change has offered proof that having a mental issue doesn't restrict someone's ability.

When someone discusses their story of mental illness, it not only benefits them but also has a rippling impact on others. People feel seen, understood, and less alone in their troubles. They come to learn that just because they have a mental condition doesn't imply they are damaged or unable. This has been vital in building a healthy discussion around mental health, one where individuals feel comfortable seeking treatment without shame.

A vital lesson these folks bring forward is the significance of keeping the body, heart, and mind healthy. Mental health is equally as crucial as physical health, yet many individuals fail to care for their mental well-being. In today's fast-paced society, we are regularly advised to exercise, eat correctly, and get enough sleep. However, how frequently are we prompted to halt and check in with our brains and emotions? The reality is that just as our bodies need care and attention, so do our brains. Seeking assistance, whether via therapy, medicine, or other types of treatment, is not only acceptable but vital.

Many individuals fear asking out for help because they feel it's a show of weakness or something to be embarrassed by. But nothing could be farther from the truth. Mental health issues may happen to everyone, regardless of their background, status, or life events. The key is recognizing when you need help and realizing that asking for it is a show of strength, not weakness. It demonstrates that you are taking ownership of your well-being and are prepared to do what it takes to recover and prosper.

One key factor that individuals frequently neglect is the requirement for expert counsel while dealing with mental health concerns. Whether it's schizophrenia, bipolar illness, depression, or anxiety, it is vital to seek competent guidance. Mental health specialists are educated to assist clients in understanding their symptoms and locating the best treatment alternatives. Treatment might vary based on the person and the illness. For some, treatment may be adequate, while others may need medication or a mix of both.

In many situations, mental health disorders are curable, and people may go on to have productive, full lives with the correct therapy. It's crucial to note that while mental health concerns may not always have a "cure" in the traditional sense, they may often be treated successfully. Treatment can help lessen symptoms, enhance the quality of life, and enable patients to follow their goals and objectives. For individuals unclear about what sort of care they need, scheduling a consultation with a mental health specialist is the first step toward recovery.

People frequently look up to prominent characters, and when those celebrities share their mental health struggles, it sends a strong message. It reminds us that mental illness does not discriminate; even people who seem to have it all together can struggle. Their tales indicate that mental illness is not a barrier to success, and it is possible to live an optimistic and productive life with the correct assistance. These notable personalities prove that with proper treatment, mental health difficulties can be controlled, and one may achieve great things, both personally and professionally.

Take, for example, the numerous celebrities, athletes, musicians, and prominent people who have talked publicly about their experiences with depression, anxiety, or other mental health disorders. Their bravery in coming out has motivated thousands more to do the same. They teach us that even if they confront their obstacles, they can still perform on stage, win games, produce art, and have a positive effect on the world. These folks are proof that mental illness is not the end of the tale; it's simply a part of the journey.

Mental health should be handled like any other health concern. Just as one would see a doctor for a broken bone or a chronic cough, one should consult a mental health specialist for mental health difficulties. Early intervention is frequently crucial in addressing mental health disorders. The sooner someone gets help, the higher their chances of finding a treatment plan that works for them. Waiting too long can sometimes make symptoms worse and make recovery more complicated. That's why it's crucial to check with a physician as soon as symptoms develop.

Therapy, medication, and other types of therapy are all legitimate alternatives for addressing mental health conditions. What works for one individual might not work for another, and that's alright. Mental health is not a one-size-fits-all issue. The most essential thing is finding what works best for you and sticking with it.

Mental illness does not have to define someone's life. With the correct therapy, individuals may achieve their objectives, find pleasure, and contribute to society in meaningful ways. Many who have battled with mental illness have gone on to achieve great things, not despite their condition but because they learned to manage it and use their experiences to fuel their growth.

There is one important thing that one needs to understand: it is not shameful to be suffering from mental illness. Little does one know that one needs prior consultation for any of their mental disorder, including schizophrenia, bipolar disorder and other related disorders, whether it's therapy, medication or any form of treatment. If famous personalities' story with mental illness proves one thing, that is, it is curable, and people can live hopeful and productive lives if only they receive proper treatment.

In addition to John Nash, Mariah Carey, Jean-Claude Van Damme and Kanye West, some other celebrities have been diagnosed with suffering from mental health-related illnesses, including bipolar disease and schizophrenia. Their stories also describe more of the perseverance required when living with these issues but also show the ability to succeed in today's demanding environment when having these problems.

Of the celebrities, one who has shared his experience with bipolar disorder is Demi Lovato, a talented singer, composer, and actor. Demi, especially, has used her influence to raise awareness about mental illness as she does not hesitate to talk about it in her own life. They told Demi she had bipolar disease after she had been battling with depression, eating disorders and substance abuse issues. She was glad to hear such information because it was a reason for her temperamental behaviour.

Demi has stated that although her episodes of depression led her to feel so helpless and alone, her episodes of mania most often meant great feelings of grandiosity and irresponsibility. By attending therapy sessions and receiving medical attention, she has enhanced the part of her that deals with it. This would not be the first time Demi used social networks to impress her fans and raise awareness of mental health issues. On this note, Due to Demi's openness, youth are significantly less likely now to stigmatize mental illness. They were traumatized by what they saw, and this continued to be a subject of her advocacy for mental health treatment, and many of her followers sought help for their problems.

Other people who have suffered from bipolar illness include Catherine Zeta-Jones. The Traffic motion picture star and a Chicago actress revealed in 2011 that she had been diagnosed with bipolar II disease. Catherine was experiencing personal stresses at the time when she was announcing this, including her husband, Michael Douglas, who had cancer. It was appreciated because she decided to share her experience and fight for mental illness to be discussed more frequently and easily, especially when it comes to working women.

Catherine was once an inspiration for how bipolar disease can be controlled by regular counselling and the use of medication, so she continues with her Hollywood life and career. Her fear of showing off her mentality has had a large impact on how mental illness is perceived in the entertainment industry, encouraging other talents to seek help and address their problems.

Another celebrity who the public knew she had bipolar disorder was Carrie Fisher. She was particularly famous for her role as the sexy Princess Leia in Star Wars. Carrie was a mental health activist and was engaged with bipolar disease and addiction throughout her life. She ensured she became an approachable person for people experiencing the same ordeal by often using humour to talk about them. Carrie has not been shy about the ups and downs that come with the struggle with mental health in her memoirs, episodes of mania and depression that often went hand in hand with substance addiction.

Carrie blazed trails in the sense that she felt free to discuss her mental condition much, as people did not talk much about mental challenges. She has lighted the way to bipolar disease, and her spirit teaches people to own their struggles and embrace them with honesty and laughter. Carrie's most valuable part of her life has been a fight for a mental health cause, and, albeit a long time since her acting career, she is loved and appreciated for her activism as well.

Lionel Aldridge is another famous person diagnosed with schizophrenia; he was a player of American football with the Packers during the 1960's. Aldridge was a key in the Packers' defensive game plan during the Packers' Super Bowl victories; however, since he retired from football, he began to show noticeable symptoms of schizophrenia. The story reveals that he suffered from the illness and had a time in his life when he had no shelter and no one around him. Aldridge only had to manage his symptoms and regain control of his life with the help of counselling and the support of his family.

Sometime later, Aldridge went on to become an advocate for mental health, sharing his own story and thus trying to raise awareness regarding schizophrenia and the struggles a person with a mental disease has to face. His work played a tremendous role in removing misconceptions about the so-called 'LOSERS' of the sports world and explaining that they have mental illnesses and that the players of the sports world are unbeatable. Aldridge's story is a dramatic illustration of the fact that while stars and athletes may have it all, they too are vulnerable to mental illness and getting care is the first step.

Vivien Leigh, a brilliant movie actress who starred in the film Gone with the Wind as Scarlett O'Hara, had bipolar illness throughout her lifetime. A lot of times, her mental health issues got in the way of her personal and work life, though she displayed extraordinary talents and was a successful actress in Hollywood. This patient reported having strong mood swings — sometimes, she could not maintain relationships nor perform acting for long. She, however, continued giving first-class performances in these conditions. These challenges firmly established her as one of the best actors in the world.

At the time of her fight against bipolar disease, there was very limited information regarding this illness, and Leigh could not get the same help and treatment as can be gotten today. Her story remains an important example of how mental illness can affect at least those who are highly successful. I think Leigh's story is a sad example of the need for mental health education and the need to embrace and support people who struggle with their mental health.

Today, the British comedian, actor, and writer Russell Brand of Sweeney Todd fame had no qualms about revealing that he has been dealing with ADHD and bipolar issues as well as addictions. Russell has stated many times just how much his mental illness affects his life, especially in the early days of his career when the mania that he suffered from led to impulsive behaviour and abuse of substances. Russell hit rock bottom and was ready to quit drinking; he went for treatment and even began meditating.

Russell takes advantage of his authority to support addiction recovery and to spread information about mental disorders. The process of his recovery has been one of his main themes. His story is a positive one for which people with severe mental disorders can make a lot of sense and may have a purpose in their lives. Russell is relevant to many people because of what they experience due to the ideas he provides humorously.

The TV persona and most widely known actor of the series Stranger Things, David Harbour, has also shared his fight against bipolar disorder. David has been quite frank about his struggles with mania and depression, most especially after his first diagnosis at a young age. Manic-depressive mood swings that were severe enough to make it impossible for David to work were common, but reckless actions and short periods of genius often accompanied his highs.

After receiving an early diagnosis of the illness, David was admitted to the hospital to commence medication and counselling. He has been very open about his struggles with deep depression, and the popularity of this information relieved a lot of fans, especially those who appreciate mature performance of characters. This is why their experience of David shows that despite mental illness, nobody can have a successful and full life if they are under appropriate treatment.

Another influential person is Brian Wilson, a songwriter and singer, the main founder of The Beach Boys band. The schizoaffective illness that is characterized by features of schizophrenia and mood disorder, including bipolar mood disorder or depression, is the disorder Brain. Infact, Brian has had depressive symptoms and has had to deal with auditory hallucinations, which have affected his personal life and his career as a musician.

Brian has endured major setbacks to help pen some of the most memorable compositions in the history of recorded music, including the legendary Pet Sounds record. That he turns his troubles into his work after work has made him one of the most influential musicians of all ages. This paper aims to provide a rather optimistic example of how creativity and mental disorder can interpenetrate and how you can persevere with your interests if only you receive the right support.

In addition to the renowned persons we've previously spoken about, there are countless more whose lives have been affected by their experiences with mental illness. These individuals come from a wide range of backgrounds—actors, musicians, athletes, and authors—all of them have encountered obstacles connected to diseases like schizophrenia or bipolar disorder. Each tale is a reminder that mental illness does not discriminate, and it affects people from all areas of life, no matter their popularity or success.

One of the most encouraging personalities to talk about mental illness openly is Stephen Fry. Fry is a British comedian, actor, writer, and broadcaster who has been unusually frank about his problems with bipolar disease. He originally announced his illness in a 2006 documentary, Stephen Fry: The Secret Life of the Manic Depressive. In the documentary, Fry investigated how his ailment had influenced his life, notably his moments of mania and sadness. Fry has reported feeling invincible during manic periods, often taking on huge projects and working relentlessly, only to be brought crashing down by severe regret. He has also spoken about the severe emotional suffering that comes with bipolar disease and how it once pushed him to try suicide.

Despite the hurdles he's experienced, Fry has persevered to enjoy an outstanding career in the entertainment sector. His humour, knowledge, and willingness to communicate freely about his mental health have made him a champion for mental health awareness. Fry's story resonates with people as he illustrates that it's possible to live a successful, full life even while managing a mental illness.

Another notable individual who has lived with schizophrenia is John Hinckley Jr., the man who attempted to shoot U.S. President Ronald Reagan in 1981. While Hinckley is recognized for his murder, his biography also demonstrates the deadly consequences of untreated mental illness. Hinckley had been diagnosed with schizophrenia, and at the time of the assassination attempt, he was battling with delusions and auditory hallucinations. His fascination with actress Jodie Foster led him to assume that by murdering the president, he would acquire her admiration. After his arrest, Hinckley was judged not guilty by reason of insanity and was sent to a mental facility, where he received long-term therapy.

Hinckley's case was a turning moment in the public's perception of mental illness and criminal justice. It attracted attention to the significance of mental illness in violent conduct and spurred questions about how society should approach those with serious psychiatric problems. Today, Hinckley is out of the hospital and living under supervision, but his tale remains a complicated illustration of the connection between mental illness, criminality, and therapy.

Another popular figure who has suffered from bipolar disorder is Maurice Benard, a well-known soap opera actor best renowned for his portrayal of Sonny Corinthos on General Hospital. Maurice has been candid about his difficulties with bipolar disorder, and his experiences have strongly informed his depiction of Sonny, a character who also lives with the same condition. Benard has remarked that his real-life experiences with mania and depression helped him bring realism to the part, and his portrayal has been commended for its accuracy in capturing the emotional highs and lows that come with bipolar disease.

Benard has been a mental health champion for many years, speaking out about the necessity of therapy and medication. He routinely shares his tale with followers, particularly those who are battling with their mental health. His transparency has made him an accessible figure for many, revealing that even people in the spotlight may battle major mental health difficulties.

Patty Duke, another performer who reached renown in the 1960s, was also diagnosed with bipolar illness. Tremendous mood swings defined Duke's life, but for many years, she didn't know the cause. It wasn't until later in life that she was fully identified, and by that time, her sickness had taken a toll on her relationships and work. Duke went on to become an outspoken champion for mental health, writing about her experiences in her autobiography, Call Me Anna, and delivering presentations about the need to diagnose and treat mental illness.

Duke's tale is particularly painful since she spent most of her life in the public glare, often appearing in films and on television while dealing with untreated bipolar disorder. Her boldness in coming up about her mental health later in life helped to raise awareness of the disease and opened the path for others in Hollywood to do the same.

Edward Honaker is another individual whose life has been impacted by schizophrenia. Though not a household name, Honaker became recognized for his photographic project, Schizophrenia: A Personal Experience. After being diagnosed with schizophrenia in his early twenties, Honaker began using photography to portray his emotions of loneliness, bewilderment, and separation from the world. His sombre black-and-white self-portraits portray the inner torment that many persons with schizophrenia endure.

Honaker's art has been extensively appreciated for its raw honesty and ability to portray the emotional and psychological suffering of living with schizophrenia. His experience reminds us that mental illness can be a source of creativity and self-expression, even as it brings enormous problems.

Another notable figure who has been honest about his mental health is David Bowie. While Bowie was never formally diagnosed with a mental condition, he regularly spoke of his difficulties with paranoia and delusions, notably throughout the 1970s. At the height of his stardom, Bowie was known for his flamboyant, larger-than-life characters like Ziggy Stardust and the Thin White Duke. However, behind the scenes, he was battling with serious mental health difficulties compounded by drug usage.

Bowie's experience underscores the relationship between mental health and creativity. His distinctive vision and pioneering music were, in part, influenced by his psychiatric challenges. Bowie typically utilized his art to explore issues of identity, alienation, and the human experience, and his desire to push boundaries has made him one of the most important artists of all time.

Similarly, Philippe Pinel, a French physician during the 18th century, played a crucial role in revolutionizing how mental disease was handled. Although he did not directly live with a mental disease, Pinel's work at psychiatric facilities in France helped alter the treatment of persons with disorders like schizophrenia. He is well known for campaigning for the humane treatment of people with a mental health condition, removing their shackles and treating them with decency and respect. His work helped pave the way for more humane approaches to mental health care, and his influence carries on in current psychiatric procedures.

Pinel's work reminds us of the significance of empathy and compassion in treating mental illness. His commitment to changing mental health treatment was innovative at the time and continues to affect how we think about and approach mental health today.

Another well-known individual who lived with bipolar disease was Ernest Hemingway, the famed American author and journalist. Hemingway's life was distinguished by times of extraordinary inventiveness and production but also by devastating spells of sadness. He suffered from drinking and finally took his own life in 1961. While Hemingway was never formally diagnosed with bipolar disorder during his lifetime, many experts feel that his conduct implies he lived with the disease.

Hemingway's writing often reflected his difficulties, with themes of despair, violence, and the quest for meaning showing in many of his works. His life is a reminder that mental illness can afflict even the most brilliant brains and that obtaining treatment is vital for managing these disorders. Hemingway's influence as a writer is evident, but his terrible conclusion also emphasizes the need to recognize mental health concerns early and give help to those in need.

Another artist whose work was strongly inspired by his mental health difficulties is Vincent van Gogh. The Dutch painter, famed for his classic paintings like Starry Night and Sunflowers, is thought to have lived with bipolar illness or maybe schizophrenia. Throughout his life, van Gogh had tremendous spurts of creativity, during which he produced some of his most renowned paintings. However, these manic periods were typically followed by severe sadness and insanity. Van Gogh's mental condition deteriorated over time, and he finally died by suicide in 1890.

Despite the hardships he experienced, van Gogh's work has had a tremendous effect on the world of art. His use of colour, brushstroke, and passion has inspired other painters and continues to be recognized today. Van Gogh's narrative is a testament to the intricate interplay between mental illness and creativity, as well as the significance of mental health awareness and treatment.

Amy Winehouse, the British singer famed for her deep vocals and popular songs like Rehab and Back to Black, also suffered from mental health challenges throughout her life. While she was never formally diagnosed with a specific ailment, Winehouse lived with addiction, depression, and anxiety, all of which culminated in her untimely death at the age of 27. Winehouse's raw talent and emotional depth made her one of the most recognized performers of her time, but her problems with mental illness and substance addiction often overshadowed her career.

Winehouse's narrative is a reminder of how tough it can be to handle mental health difficulties, especially in the public glare. Despite her enormous skill, she was unable to acquire the care she needed in time, resulting in her premature death. Winehouse's impact as a performer is evident, but her life also serves as a warning story about the perils of untreated mental illness and addiction.

Each of these individuals—whether diagnosed with schizophrenia, bipolar disorder, or other mental health conditions—has made a lasting influence on the world via their work and their personal stories. Their stories indicate that mental illness does not have to restrict a person's potential, but they also underscore the significance of getting treatment and support. Mental health difficulties are profoundly personal, and the journey to healing is different for everyone. Still, the unifying thread in all of these stories is resilience—the capacity to continue moving ahead despite the hurdles.

As society grows increasingly aware of mental health disorders, the tales of renowned persons who have struggled with these diseases are vital in breaking down stigma and inspiring others to get assistance. Whether via their work, campaigning, or personal experiences, these individuals have contributed to a broader knowledge of mental illness

and the significance of compassion and support. Their legacies continue to inspire and remind us that mental health is an integral component of the human experience.

These are real stories from famous people who have schizophrenia, bipolar disorder and other mental diseases that prove that people with such diseases are also able to be talented and achieve something. Despite all these human interest stories, these people have triumphed in overcoming these challenges; they have also offered inspiration and created awareness. It sheds light on their condition and proves that it is possible to go through lifelong mental illness with the right care to avoid as much stigma for the condition as possible and to encourage other people to seek treatment. They also teach about tolerance, understanding, and raising awareness that mental health is just as important as physical health.

Approximately 19% of the world's adult population lives with a mental illness, so it remains of paramount importance to continue more efforts to eliminate barriers that stand in the way of people receiving the necessary treatment. People with mental illness do not have limitations in their lives; Kanye West, Mariah Carey, Jean-Claude Van Damme, John Nash, Demi Lovato, Catherine Zeta-Jones, Carrie Fisher, Lionel Aldridge, Vivien Leigh, Russell Brand, David Harbour, and Brian Wilson. These individuals have proved unyielding and tenacious, and discussions on mental health or the relevance of seeking help whenever the need arises are still elicited by these personalities.

This particular article, the present world, which is slow to open up further discourses on the issue, is an important one to remind readers that everyone is different. However, it's crucial to understand that in some situations, people may start with other conditions, which is why it is possible for them to at least try to move past this kind of situation and, if needed, ask for help. The factors involving Kanye, Mariah, Van Damme, and Nash prove that one can be successful and not be mentally sick, and vice versa, and the three aspects of knowledge, support, and willpower help overcome various mental health problems.

In conclusion, bipolar disorder is a serious mental health condition that can be challenging to manage. With the right combination of treatment, lifestyle changes, and strategies for self-care however, it is possible to lead a fulfilling life despite its challenges. When individuals are supported by a strong network of family and friends, they can find hope in even the most difficult times. We must all do our part to ensure those suffering from bipolar disorder receive the help and support they need. Together we can make sure that no one has to go through this journey alone.

Rules of different states of how they incarcerate the mentally challenged

States in the US differ greatly in how people with mental illness or developmental impairments are treated and imprisoned. States typically adhere to both national policy and state-specific laws. Depending on whether someone is found mentally incompetent, not guilty by reason of insanity, or if mental health problems develop while they are behind bars, there are additional distinct pathways. General guidelines on how various governments handle these matters under different legal systems are provided:

Federal Guidelines

The Americans with Disabilities Act (ADA) and the Civil Rights of Institutionalized Persons Act (CRIPA) in particular mandate that states provide convicts with mental illnesses with appropriate care and reasonable accommodations. The ruling in Olmstead v. L.C. (1999) by the Supreme Court also mandated that, when appropriate, states place people with mental disorders in community settings as opposed to institutions.

Civil Commitment Laws

A court-ordered treatment program for individuals with severe mental illness—typically in a psychiatric institution rather than a prison—is known as "civil commitment." States have different laws on this, however most of them include provisions for:

- **Involuntary Commitment:**

A person may be admitted to a mental health hospital if they represent a risk to themselves or others. Due process, which usually entails a court hearing and a mental health professional evaluation, must be followed by the state.

Examples:

• **California:** If someone poses a risk to oneself or others due to a mental condition, they may be placed under a 72-hour psychiatric hold under the state's Lanterman-Petris-Short (LPS) Act.

• **New York:** When an individual cannot take care of themselves or poses a risk to others, the Mental Hygiene Law permits involuntary hospitalization.

• **Texas:** Under the Mental Health Code, those who pose an immediate risk may be placed in emergency detention; a professional evaluation is required, and a hearing for long-term commitment is required.

Incarceration vs. Hospitalization for Mental Illness

States usually make a distinction between those who are mentally incompetent and mentally ill. The seriousness of the offense and the individual's mental state are the main determinants of whether they be booked into a jail or psychiatric institution.

→ Competency to Stand Trial

• **Psychiatric facilities:** are usually used to treat and stabilize mentally incompetent people who are unable to comprehend the charges against them or take part in their defense. After being deemed competent again, they might go on trial.

Example:

• **Florida:** The law permits the placement of defendants in state mental hospitals for treatment if they are found to be incompetent to stand trial.

→ Not Guilty by Reason of Insanity (NGRI)

• Instead of being committed to jail, defendants judged to be NGRI are typically sent to safe mental health facilities. The severity of the disease and the offense may affect how long you have to stay.

Example:

• **Virginia:** Those found to be NGRI are committed to a mental health facility for assessment and treatment, with periodic court evaluations of their progress, in accordance with Virginia Code § 19.2-182.2.

Diversion Programs and Specialized Courts

Numerous states have established mental health courts and diversionary programs with the goal of treating mentally ill people rather than locking them up. These programs, which frequently include probation, treatment requirements, and routine court monitoring, include cooperation between the legal and mental health systems.

Examples:

• **Ohio:** This state runs mental health courts, which send mentally ill defendants to treatment facilities rather than jails.

•**New Jersey:**Provides a Jail Diversion Program designed to divert people with severe mental illnesses from the criminal justice system and place them in suitable treatment facilities.

Conditions of Confinement for Mentally Ill Inmates

States have different policies on the treatment and conditions of incarceration for mentally ill people. Laws in many jurisdictions mandate that jails offer mental health care. The level and type of care might, however, vary.

→ **Mental Health Units in Prisons**

Within their jail systems, some states have specialized wings or sections reserved for the mentally sick. These units might provide monitoring, therapy, and specialized care.

Example:

- **Illinois:**The state offers therapeutic treatment for prisoners with serious mental health concerns through mental health facilities housed in a number of its prisons.

→ **Solitary Confinement**

Many states have come under fire for confining people with mental illnesses in solitary confinement, which has been shown to exacerbate their conditions. A number of states have passed legislation limiting the use of solitary confinement for prisoners who are mentally ill.

Example:

- **Colorado:** In response to public criticism and lawsuits, the state drastically reduced the use of solitary confinement for prisoners suffering from mental diseases.

Post-Incarceration Supervision and Treatment

States differ in how they handle continuous mental health treatment and post-incarceration supervision for mentally ill people who have been released from prison.

→ **Community Reentry Programs**

To assist mentally ill people in reintegrating into society after being released from prison, some states have created specialized reentry programs that guarantee they have access to housing, mental health care, and other essential services.

Example:

• **California:**Community-based programs that help mentally ill people transition from jail to community living are funded by the state's Mental Health Services Act.

→ Conditional Release

Some states allow conditional release in situations where an individual has been committed to a mental health facility following an NGRI finding if the individual shows appreciable progress. They might need to continue receiving treatment and be watched over.

Lawsuits and Consent Decrees

Consent decrees, which mandate that the state improve conditions or face penalties, have resulted from lawsuits filed in various states over insufficient mental health care provided to prisoners.

Example:

• Alabama: In Braggs v. Dunn (2017), a federal judge declared that the state's jail mental health care system was "horrendously inadequate" and mandated extensive modifications.

Variations by State: Mental Health Treatment in Jails

Compared to state-run prisons, many locally controlled jails provide fewer mental health treatments. There are programs in place in a few states to enhance local mental health screening, treatment, and diversion.

Example:

• **Louisiana:** Although local jails in Louisiana have come under fire for providing subpar mental health treatment, new legislation is attempting to improve staff training and expand access to psychiatric services.

The rules and approaches to incarcerating individuals with mental health challenges vary across U.S. states, often influenced by local policies, available resources, and legal frameworks. Some states have established diversion programs aimed at keeping mentally ill individuals out of traditional jails and prisons by redirecting them to treatment facilities. For example, states like California, Texas, and New York have mental health courts that work specifically with offenders who have mental health issues, offering alternatives to incarceration such as treatment programs, counseling, and supervision. These courts aim to reduce recidivism by addressing the root causes of the behavior linked to mental illness.

Other states have implemented crisis intervention teams (CITs) within law enforcement agencies. CITs are designed to train police officers on how to handle situations involving individuals with mental illness, emphasizing de-escalation and referral to mental health services instead of arrest. States such as Ohio and Florida are known for adopting robust CIT models that encourage partnerships between law enforcement, mental health providers, and community organizations.

In states without well-developed diversion or treatment systems, mentally ill individuals may be incarcerated in general population prisons or jails, where they often lack access to appropriate care. In these settings, individuals with mental health conditions may be placed in solitary confinement as a way to manage their symptoms or behavior, which can exacerbate their mental health issues. Some states, such as Illinois and North Carolina, have faced lawsuits and advocacy pressure to improve conditions for mentally ill inmates, leading to reforms like enhanced mental health screenings and increased access to psychiatric care in prisons.

Additionally, federal laws like the Americans with Disabilities Act (ADA) and rulings such as the U.S. Supreme Court's decision in Olmstead v. L.C. (1999) require states to provide appropriate accommodations for mentally ill individuals and offer community-based treatment when possible. However, the degree to which states comply with these mandates varies widely based on resources, political will, and public advocacy efforts.

The incarceration of individuals with mental health challenges varies widely across states, with significant differences in how the criminal justice system interacts with and treats these individuals. In some states, mental health diversion programs aim to prevent mentally ill individuals from being incarcerated in the first place. These programs often work in conjunction with law enforcement and the courts to redirect offenders toward community-based mental health services. For example, states like New York and California have established mental health courts that allow judges to offer treatment alternatives instead of prison sentences. These courts assess whether an individual's criminal behavior is related to their mental illness and then determine whether a specialized treatment plan, including therapy, medication, or supervised housing, might be more appropriate than incarceration.

Another approach seen in some states is the use of Crisis Intervention Teams (CIT), which are composed of law enforcement officers trained specifically to recognize and respond to individuals experiencing a mental health crisis. Ohio and Florida are two states that have developed robust CIT programs, where officers work in close collaboration with mental health professionals to ensure that individuals in crisis are diverted to care rather than arrested. These teams are often dispatched when 911 calls involve someone with a known or suspected mental illness. The goal is to reduce the likelihood of arrest and ensure the individual gets appropriate mental health support, helping to avoid the criminalization of mental illness.

In contrast, many states still lack comprehensive diversion or mental health intervention programs, meaning mentally ill individuals are frequently incarcerated in general population settings. Jails and prisons in these states may lack the resources to provide adequate mental health treatment, and in some cases, individuals are placed in solitary confinement as a way to manage symptoms or behavior. This practice can severely exacerbate their condition. States like Illinois and North Carolina have faced legal challenges and public scrutiny over the treatment of mentally ill inmates, with advocates pushing for reforms to limit the use of solitary confinement and improve access to mental health care within correctional facilities. As a result of these efforts, some prisons have begun offering more consistent psychiatric evaluations and treatment options for inmates, although the quality and availability of care can still vary.

Additionally, federal law plays a role in shaping how states manage the incarceration of individuals with mental health challenges. The Americans with Disabilities Act (ADA) mandates that individuals with disabilities, including mental illness, receive reasonable accommodations while incarcerated. Similarly, the Supreme Court's Olmstead v. L.C. decision requires states to provide treatment for individuals with mental illness in the least restrictive setting possible, which can include community-based services rather than institutionalization. However, compliance with these laws is not uniform, and enforcement often depends on the state's resources and political climate. States with strong mental health advocacy groups or those facing lawsuits may be more likely to implement comprehensive reforms, while others lag behind, leaving individuals with mental illness to face incarceration without appropriate care.

In many cases, the experience of mentally ill individuals in the criminal justice system reflects broader societal gaps in mental health services. Some states have responded by increasing funding for community-based mental health services and investing in mental health training for law enforcement and corrections officers. Other states, however, continue to rely heavily on the prison system as a default solution for managing individuals with untreated mental health issues, contributing to a cycle of recidivism and worsening mental health outcomes for incarcerated individuals. The disparity between states in handling mentally ill offenders highlights the uneven access to treatment and support across the country, with some regions offering progressive alternatives to incarceration and others perpetuating harmful practices that deepen the criminalization of mental illness.

The treatment of individuals with mental health challenges within the criminal justice system is shaped by a wide range of practices across different states, reflecting varying degrees of emphasis on treatment, rehabilitation, and punishment. In many cases, these individuals are subject to diversion programs that aim to steer them away from incarceration and toward mental health treatment. These programs can intervene at various points in the legal process, including before arrest, after arrest but before trial, or during sentencing. States such as California and New York have developed mental health courts that are specifically designed to handle cases involving mentally ill offenders. These courts recognize that mental illness often plays a central role in criminal behavior and offer tailored interventions such as mandatory participation in therapy, medication adherence programs, or substance abuse treatment. The goal is not only to prevent the individual from returning to jail but also to address the underlying issues contributing to their criminal activity. Successful completion of these programs may result in reduced charges or even case dismissal, offering a more compassionate and effective solution than incarceration.

In states like Ohio and Georgia, crisis intervention teams (CIT) have been implemented to prevent arrests of mentally ill individuals in crisis situations. These teams consist of law enforcement officers who receive specialized training in de-escalation techniques and the recognition of mental health symptoms. The CIT model seeks to divert individuals experiencing a mental health crisis away from jail and into treatment facilities or hospitals. Officers are trained to work with mental health professionals in their communities to identify and direct individuals toward appropriate services, often preventing unnecessary jail time. Florida, for example, has made significant efforts to adopt the CIT model statewide, ensuring that law enforcement agencies are better equipped to handle mental health-related calls for service. By providing officers with the skills to manage these situations without resorting to arrest, states that implement CITs can reduce the strain on both their criminal justice and healthcare systems, as well as improve outcomes for individuals with mental illness.

Despite the existence of diversion programs and CITs in some states, a significant number of individuals with mental health challenges still find themselves incarcerated. In many states, jails and prisons are ill-equipped to meet the needs of mentally ill inmates, leading to inadequate care and, in some cases, harmful practices such as the use of solitary confinement. Solitary confinement is often used as a form of punishment or control when individuals with mental illness exhibit disruptive behavior, but it has been shown to exacerbate conditions such as depression, anxiety, and psychosis. Advocacy groups and civil rights organizations have brought attention to these practices, leading to reforms in some states. For instance, lawsuits in

Illinois and North Carolina have resulted in court-mandated improvements to the mental health services provided to incarcerated individuals. These reforms have included better access to psychiatric care, increased staffing of mental health professionals within correctional facilities, and the development of treatment plans for inmates with serious mental health issues.

Federal law also plays an important role in shaping how states address the incarceration of mentally ill individuals. The Americans with Disabilities Act (ADA) requires that individuals with disabilities, including mental health conditions, be provided with reasonable accommodations, which can include access to psychiatric care, medication, and therapy while incarcerated. However, compliance with the ADA varies widely among states and even within individual correctional facilities. Some prisons have been criticized for failing to provide adequate accommodations, leading to lawsuits and calls for reform. The Olmstead v. L.C. decision by the U.S. Supreme Court further mandates that states provide mental health services in the least restrictive setting possible, which often means community-based treatment rather than institutionalization. Yet, despite this ruling, many states still struggle to provide sufficient community-based mental health services, leaving individuals with mental illness to cycle in and out of the criminal justice system.

In states with limited mental health resources, mentally ill individuals are more likely to face arrest and incarceration, often for minor offenses such as trespassing, disorderly conduct, or public intoxication. This is particularly common among homeless populations, where untreated mental illness and substance abuse frequently lead to interactions with law enforcement. Without adequate diversion programs, these individuals may be incarcerated for extended periods, during which their mental health conditions can worsen due to the lack of appropriate treatment. In some cases, inmates with severe mental health conditions are placed in solitary confinement or subjected to other punitive measures, which can lead to further deterioration of their mental state.

Some states are attempting to address these issues by increasing funding for mental health services and expanding diversion programs. For example, Washington state has invested in community mental health programs aimed at reducing the number of mentally ill individuals entering the criminal justice system. These programs focus on providing services such as housing, case management, and access to mental health professionals, helping individuals manage their conditions and avoid interactions with law enforcement. Other states are exploring similar models, recognizing that treating mental illness as a public health issue rather than a criminal justice issue can lead to better outcomes for both individuals and society.

However, not all states have been able to implement these changes effectively, often due to budget constraints, political resistance, or a lack of coordination between criminal justice and mental health systems. In these states, jails and prisons continue to serve as de facto mental health facilities, despite being poorly equipped to provide the necessary care. The result is often a revolving door, where individuals with untreateds mental illness are repeatedly arrested, incarcerated, and released, only to find themselves back in the criminal justice system due to a lack of support and services. This cycle not only harms the individuals involved but also places a significant burden on state and local resources.

Overall, the approaches to incarcerating and treating mentally ill individuals in the U.S. are highly inconsistent, with some states prioritizing diversion and treatment while others rely heavily on incarceration. As a result, the experience of individuals with mental illness within the criminal justice system can vary dramatically depending on where they live, highlighting the need for more uniform and compassionate policies across the country.

State-by-state variations exist in the criminal justice system's treatment of mentally ill people, which are impacted by local policies, resources, and perspectives on mental health. While many states have made progress in creating mental health courts and diversionary programs, others still struggle to provide enough care and make sure that people with mental illnesses receive the treatment they require rather than just being locked up.

CONCLUSION

The world has got you. I want you always to remember that and try to stay positive. It is just a stumbling block in your life, and I believe that you can overcome this. You are not alone, there are thousands of survivors out there, and you could be one of them. You need to take that first step. Now, I know it is not easy, but you have got to try. You are the master of your mind and not the other way round. We cannot heal you or be there for you if you are unwilling to take a stand for yourself to get better.

I read a post online, and I think we all need to adopt that thinking. I quote: "I will always be there for anyone who needs me. I will always be a helping hand or a listening ear because I know what it is like to believe that no one cares. I know what it is like to feel alone, suffocated in your thoughts. I know how just one person can change someone else's life. I am here for anyone that needs me to prove that compassion still exists. I am here for you."

For those that are here because of a loved one, I want you to understand that you must be severely patient with them. It is not fun dealing with someone else's mood swings or their rejection of your offer to help. Please understand that they are confused and feel lost and alone and that your impatience might make them withdraw from you. So it would help if you treated them with kindness, understanding, and patience.

If you are here for yourself, I truly wish you the best, and I hope you always convince yourself that you are not the rain. And you never will be. Everything will fall into place once you believe in yourself and reach out your hand. And always consider your loved ones' feelings and understand that they are here for you and always want the best for you. But you must help them be there for you. I hope your healing comes easy.

If you are here for the knowledge, I hope you have learned a lot and put it to good use.

Thank you all for being a part of this journey. I wish you the best.

www.ingramcontent.com/pod-product-compliance
Lightning Source LLC
LaVergne TN
LVHW050542160826
845677LV00011B/2149
* 9 7 9 8 8 9 6 9 1 0 0 4 6 *